VOLUME

1

INSURANCE ADJUSTING
Real Property Claims

ISBN-13: 978-1-933039-39-8

Library of Congress -in-Publication Data

Printed in the United States of America

10 9 8 7 6 5 4 3 2 1

The enclosed material is designed for educational purposes only. Each State may have different certification and specific guidelines. Please refer to your State for additional and future information. The information contained herein is considered correct at the time of creation but laws and regulations are updated frequently and the reader assumes the responsibility for confirming current regulations and applicable data. The publisher and author make no warranty as to the success of the individuals using the material contained herein. The publisher and author make no warranty as to any action taken by any individual completing this program. The reader is responsible for the appropriate use of the materials and information provided. This publication is designed to provide accurate and authoritative information concerning the subject matter. All material is sold with the understanding that neither the author nor the publisher guarantees the actions of any individual making use of the inclusions. Neither the author nor the publisher is rendering a legal opinion, accounting recommendation or other professional service. If legal advice or other expert assistance is desired, the services of a legal professional or other individual should be sought. The applicable publically released forms, disclosures and notices are generated from public domain. Copyright law does apply to all intellectual materials and all rights under said law are reserved b y the copyright owner.

Coursework is available at special quantity discounts to use as premiums and sales promotions within corporate or private training programs. To obtain information or inquire about availability please write to Director, PO Box 1, Hollidaysburg, PA 16648.

NOTICE

INSURANCE ADJUSTING

Real Property Claims

CHAPTER 9

APPENDIX

Congratulations on your decision to gain the skills that will enable you to become a top insurance claims adjuster. The position of an insurance adjuster requires attention to detail, critical thinking skills, exceptional judgment, decision-making capability, and an understanding of your responsibility to both the homeowner and the insurance company.

As a property claims adjuster, you will apply the knowledge, tools, and skills necessary to ensure that property claims settlements are processed speedily and that settlement is fair to all parties. You will assist people in navigating the many responsibilities relating to a personal property claim while providing the support necessary to assist the insured in recovering from a difficult period in their lives. The professionalism you will bring to the field helps to ensure that the insurer is protected from false, expanded, and fraudulent claims.

Positions within the field of insurance claims are stable, challenging, and present an exceptional opportunity for personal and career growth.

Individuals and business owners purchase insurance to help protect them against losses that may occur due to events beyond their control. When a loss occurs, the policyholder will seek monetary assistance from the insurance company that has issued a policy that protects their home or business. When a loss occurs, the insurance claims adjuster's primary duties are to investigate and evaluate each element of the claim, negotiate claim payment settlements and ensure that the claim process is closed in a manner that is fair and just for all parties.

The most common positions available to the insurance claim adjuster relate to home or automobile claims. This coursework will focus primarily on the home coverage segment of the insurance industry, but the claims processes will be similar among all claims adjustment positions.

You will be responsible for

- Evaluating the policy components

- Examining policy coverage's

- Validating the loss cause

- Determining possible loss exclusions

- Assessing dollar values to the loss

- Analyzing all of the data gathered during the claim investigation

- Generating a findings and recommendations report

- Ensuring work standards

- Maintaining expense ratios

- Negotiating and overseeing loss settlement functions

- Minimizing fraudulent activity

- Maximizing the protection afforded to both the insured and the insurer

A position as a career insurance claim adjuster is among the most rewarding and challenging offered within the insurance industry. You will assist individuals in recovering from challenging and emotional losses while maintaining a professionalism that protects the insurer.

This training will lead you through the fundamentals of property claims adjusting by building your knowledge from an entry level understanding of property claims to the realm of Insurance Claim Adjusting Professional.

Each chapter within the training series builds upon the knowledge that you have gained in the previous chapters. Some areas of the adjusting profession will be touched upon in a general manner and then further defined within a later chapter. It is important that you gain a comprehensive understanding of the inclusions of each segment of training prior to proceeding to the next chapter.

Each segment of the training coursework has a corresponding workbook program that you should use to test your knowledge of the contents. It is important that you complete the self-test worksheets to ensure that you are gaining the necessary knowledge, tools, and skills that you need to become an exceptional insurance claims adjuster.

The career opportunity presented to you as an insurance claims adjuster enables you to become a well-respected professional within your community. You will provide essential support to the individuals within your community during a time that is, potentially, one of the most traumatic and emotional in their lives. This coursework will provide you with the fundamental knowledge that you need to understand the industry surrounding insurance adjusting, the role that you will play within that industry, and the practices that you must follow to reach an equitable settlement for each party of a claim.

At the end of the coursework is a chapter that will assist you in defining the strengths inherent to your personality. This information will enable you to isolate the characteristics of your personality that will assist you in your adjusting career. You will gain an understanding of how you react in different situations, the support systems you must put in place to maximize your career potential and the methods that you may employ to gain the necessary support you need to achieve career success.

Gaining an understanding of your inherent career strengths, situational responses, and necessary career support, helps you to expand your potential and become a top adjuster within the industry.

Ensuring that you have the solid foundation of knowledge and tools necessary to adjust claims competently and reach an equitable settlement, helps you to maximize your potential for long-term career success.

Defining a Claim

An insurance claim is a request by an insured to receive monetary compensation for a loss event that occurs with regard to the property covered under an insurance policy issued by the company for which you work.

You must gain a comprehensive understanding of the insurance industry, policy form and inclusions, and claims handling processes. This understanding will enable you to complete the adjusting functions essential to the fair settlement of the claim.

You will use these skills to determine

- that the claim is being brought by an individual who has an insurable interest in the damaged property

- if the loss is caused by an event or peril that is covered under the policy

- whether there is a likelihood of fraudulent activity relating to the claim

- the equitable value of the claim that will enable fair settlement

- if limitations exist within the policy coverage that may limit or nullify the claim

- the best processes to employ to reach a claim resolution and finalize the settlement negotiation

- the total costs of any construction, restoration or repairs necessary as a result of the peril

Each of these determinations constitutes a portion of your functions as a claims adjuster. Each element is critical to the overall adjusting process and to your success as an insurance claims adjuster. You should ensure that you gain the knowledge, tools, and skills that you need to complete each essential function of your position.

The first step to gaining the knowledge, tools, and skills that you need is to gain a general understanding of the typical claim process.

GENERAL CLAIM PROCESS

A claim will be opened when an insured or an agent for the insured reports the loss to your office. Each insurance claim situation will be different. The event that instigated the claim and the amount of the claim will vary depending on the specific situation.

The first action that will occur when an insured reports a claim is the initial valuation. If the claim is minimal in cost, the investigation processes may be limited or non-existent. If a claim is more elaborate, the investigation and adjusting processes will require the services of a claims investigator or adjuster.

```
                    ┌─────────────────────────┐
                    │   INSURED REPORTS LOSS  │
                    └─────────────────────────┘
```

Claim Evaluation Limited Claim	Claim Evaluation Complex Claim
Internal Settlement	Adjuster Assignment

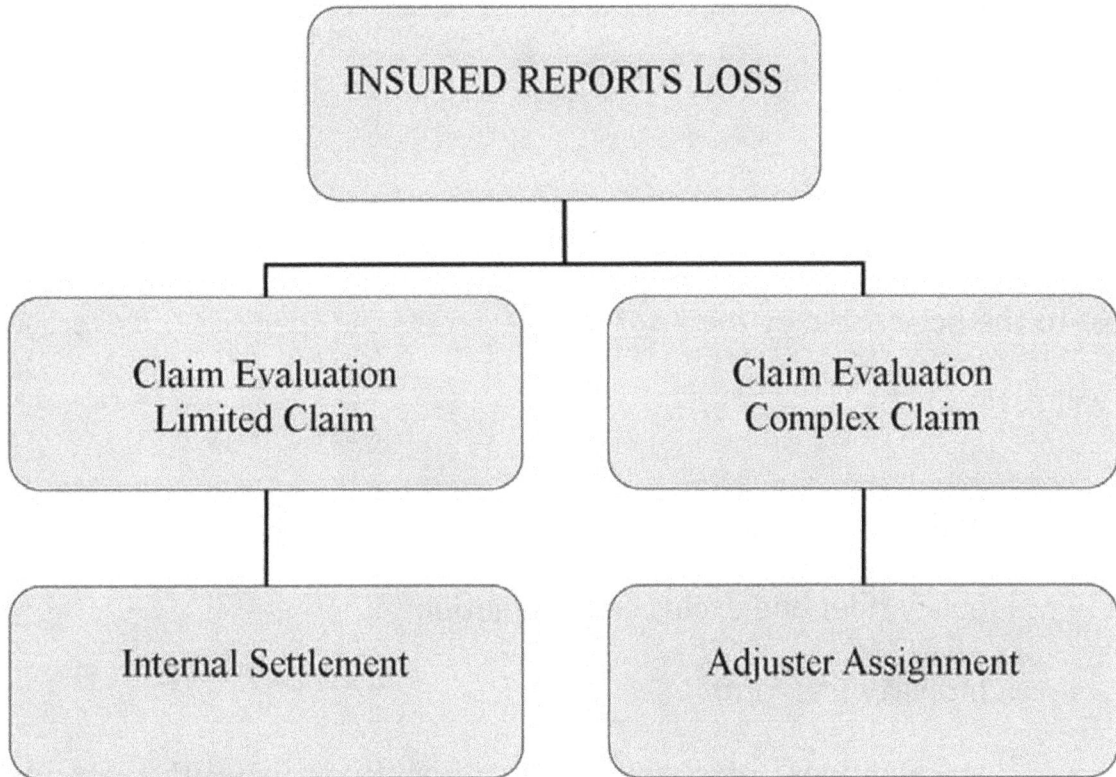

Figure 1:1 Initial Loss Report Settlement Assignment

When the claims department receives notice of a loss event, they will assign the claim to an adjuster. This assignment will typically be based upon the geographical region of the claim. If the claim is more extensive, a special adjuster with advanced skills may be assigned.

When you receive a claim assignment, you will be given basic information regarding the claim such as the

- date of the loss

- type of loss

- insured contact information

- loss location

- policy data

- binder information

The claims management representative or independent insurance agent who takes the initial claim report will complete a property loss form. This form will be provided to you as part of the adjusting assignment. You will also have access to the policy held by the insured that details the specifics of coverage.

You will review

- policy inclusions

- policy rider and exclusion information

- property loss form

- any additional information that is provided to you with the assignment

These items will provide you with the foundation that you will require to create the claims file and begin the adjusting processes.

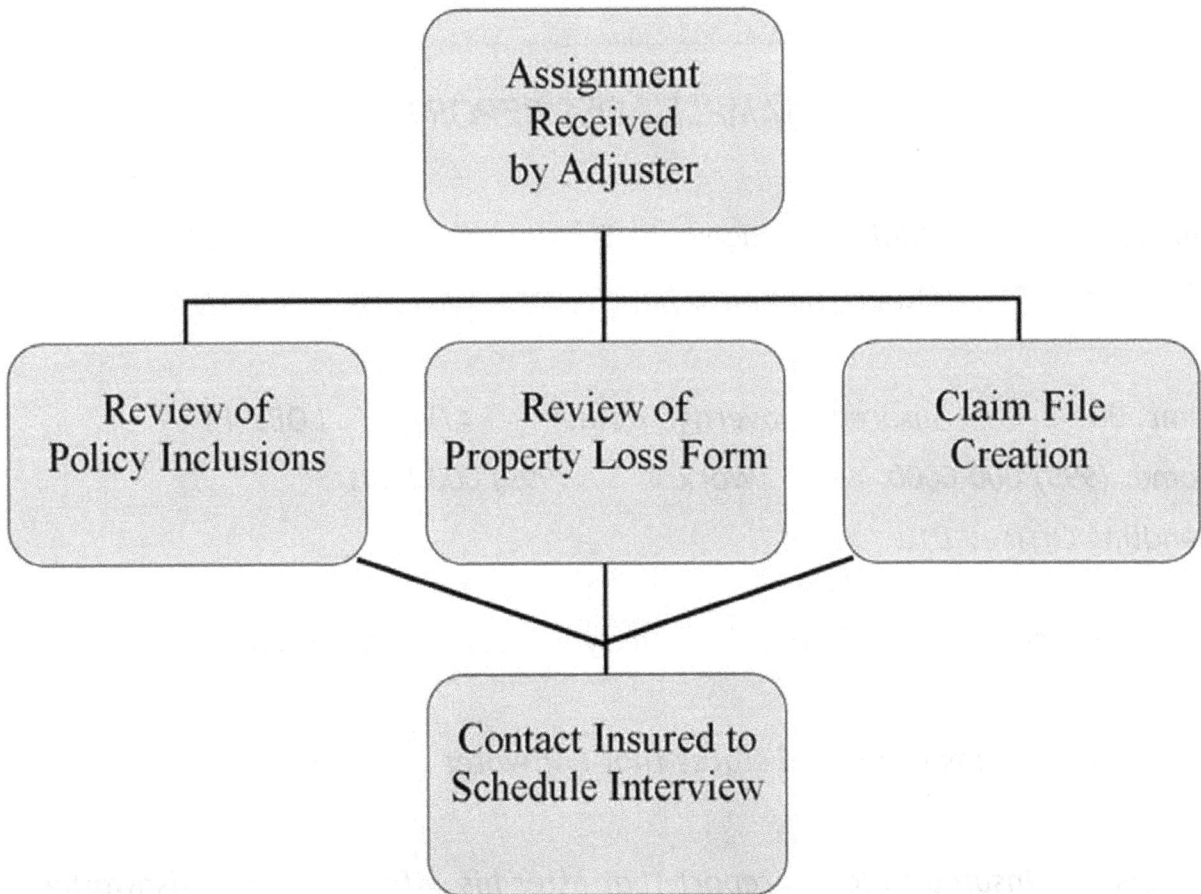

Figure 1:2   Adjusters Preparatory Actions

After you have reviewed the claim details, policy, and loss report, you will contact the insured to schedule a meeting. During this meeting you will

- assess the claim

- discuss the parameters of the insurance policy coverage

- define the processes that will occur during the settlement of the claim

- answer any questions the insured may have in relationship to the claim, coverage, and settlement

SAMPLE LOSS REPORT

06/17/20XX   Claims Management System   Clm: 010100115950

  8:07 am   Other Than Auto Loss Report Cat: HL   RR: 04

Clmt: 001   Insured: Coverage Holder   A/W: Y LOB: HP

Home: (999) 000-0000   Work: (999) 000-0001

Handling Office: 010

Unit: Primary 111   Insured's Primary Residence   Any City   USA

Summary: Claimant insured states that hot water tank failed
Sub?   Y

Details: Insured called to report that after his wife turned the dishwasher,
            the water heater (located in the basement) apparently failed,
            draining all of the water out of the tank. The tank subsequently
            overheated and caught a basket of clothing on a nearby laundry
            table on fire.

Police/Fire: Any City Fire Department   Policy: HO Broad Cover

Property Info: Primary Residence, Year of Construction 1974, Frame,

Protection Class A

Property is within 500 feet of a fire hydrant and within 3 miles of a responding
fire department

Coverage is provided only if a specific amount of insurance is shown.

Section I - Property Protection   Amount of Insurance

      Dwelling $ 191,000

      Other Structures $ 19,100

      Personal Property $ 98,250

      Loss of Use   Loss sustained not to exceed
                                            12 consecutive months

Section II - Home and Family Liability Protection

      Personal Liability- each occurrence $ 300,000

      Medical Payments- each person $ 1,000

Section III – Deductible $ 250

Section IV – Applicable Forms

20XX HP-ST, UF-8706, UF-6522, UF-9012, HP-FN, UF4044, HP-AAN, HP-BD

Section V - Loss Payee

Primary Residence – Mortgage   Primary Residence - 2nd Mortgage

First Mortgage Company Details   Second Mortgage Company Details

NO BUSINESS PURSUITS ARE CONDUCTED AT THE PREMISES, EXCEPT AS FOLLOWS:
    None

Additional Coverage:

Premises Alarm System – Type 2

    Replacement Cost Settlement – Personal Property

    Multi-Policy Discount Applies

Figure 1:3   Sample Loss Report

The loss statement summary will provide you with basic details regarding the claim. These details enable you to pre-screen the claim for specific coverage's, interested parties covered by the policy, policy status, coverage limitations and other information that will be entered into your claim management files and act as a guide as you complete the adjusting process.

06/17/20XX	*Claims Management System*	*Clm: 010100115950*
8:07 am	*Other Than Auto Loss Report*	*Cat: HL RR: 04*

Figure 1:4 Loss Summary Report Header Information

The header of the loss report will contain information illustrating the date and time of the receipt of the loss report. This date and time on the loss report indicate the time that the insured made contact to report the loss, not the time of the loss event.

COVERAGE AND LOSS DATE AND TIME

This policy applies to losses that occur during the policy period. The policy period is shown on the **Declarations**. Unless otherwise specified on the **Declarations**, the policy period begins and ends at 12:01 A.M., Standard Time at the stated address of the **Named Insured**.

Figure 1:5 Coverage Extraction Sample – Coverage Date and Time

It is important that you confirm that the coverage is in effect when you receive a loss report.

The coverage declarations will detail the exact coverage period and the loss report should confirm that the premium is up to date and the property coverage is in effect at the time that you open the case file.

If the policy has lapsed, you will refer the file back to the senior adjuster for review and coverage confirmation.

You should use the claim number assigned to the claim when you create your initial claim form. This claim number will be used as a designator for all documents relating to the adjusting process.

Clmt: 001   Insured: Coverage Holder   A/W: Y LOB: HP

Home: (999) 000-0000   Work: (999) 000-0001

Handling Office: 010

Figure 1:6 Initial Loss Report Claimant Information

The contact information of the insured who reported the loss event will be provided. The reporting individual may not be the primary policyholder. You should ensure that the primary interested insured is designated as your primary contact for the adjusting process.

INSURABLE INTEREST

Upon review of the loss summary, you must determine if the individual making the claim actually holds insurable interest under the policy. Insurable interest refers to those individuals who are covered directly by the policy or those granted secondary rights under the policy.

The ability to make a claim and receive payment under a policy is not limited to only the owner of the property. Other individuals beyond the property owner may be entitled to payment under the policy.

Property Owners, Secondary Occupants, Joint Owners, and those who hold a security interest in the property may all hold insurable interest under the policy, even when they are not expressly named within the policy. It is important that you interview the claimant to determine if secondary interests, security interests, or property liens exist, that may require third party approval or payment during the claims process. The insured should provide you with information about secondary claimants who may have suffered a loss because of the covered peril during your initial interview.

Anyone who holds an interest in the property should be protected under the policy. It is the responsibility of those who hold this interest to ensure that they receive all of the benefits of coverage. The insured is responsible for ensuring that their interest is protected in any settlement of the claim. You should review the loss report and policy entries to confirm the specific interests disclosed on these documents. The insured will confirm and elaborate on this information during the insured interview.

---

(10) Mortgage Clause

Loss under *Dwelling Coverage* or *Other Structures Coverage* shall be payable to the mortgagees named on the **Declarations**, to the extent of their interest and in order of precedence.
Our Duties

We Will:

1.   Protect the mortgagee's interests in an insured building. This protection will not be invalidated by any act or neglect by **anyone we protect,** any breach of

---

warranty, increase in hazard, change of ownership, or foreclosure if the mortgagee has no knowledge of these conditions.

2.   give mortgagee 30 days prior notice if we cancel or refuse to continue this policy;

3.   give mortgage notice if **you** cancel this policy.

Figure 1:7   Extraction Sample - Mortgage Clause

The most common secondary interest relates to those interested parties who hold a mortgage or another lien against the property. These liens transfer a specific interest in the property making the lien holder an interested party in any claim action. The interest of a lien holder is different that that of the primary insured. Most policies will incorporate a specific clause that details the coverage afforded to a mortgage holder.

It is important that you gain an understanding of the interest held by a mortgagee to a property. The mortgage holder has the right to receive notice any changes to the policy terms, any action that results in coverage cancellation, or any event that results in a loss claim at the security location. The processing office will send standard notifications of policy term changes or cancellation. If the loss assignment contains a mortgagee or second interested party, you should contact the processing office to confirm that the correct notices have been provided to these secondary parties.

The mortgage holder has the right to bring a claim under the policy separate from the claim of the named insured. This separation of rights ensures that the actions of the insured or a denial of claims rights to the insured does not alter the ability of the mortgage holder to gain rights under the claims process.

```
                                          ┌─────────────────┐
                                          │    Primary      │
                                          │    Insured      │
                                          └─────────────────┘
                 ┌────────────────────────┐
                 │    Lien Holder         │
                 │  Secondary Interest    │
                 └────────────────────────┘
```

Secondary interest to insured requiring the restoration of the property to original condition to maintain debt security	If primary insured is denied coverage then the maximum settlement interest becomes equal to the amount of the lien

Denial of claim The primary insured no longer retains coverage but the secondary insured position remains intact	Settlement will restore the position of primary insured to pre-loss circumstances up to the maximum limits of coverage

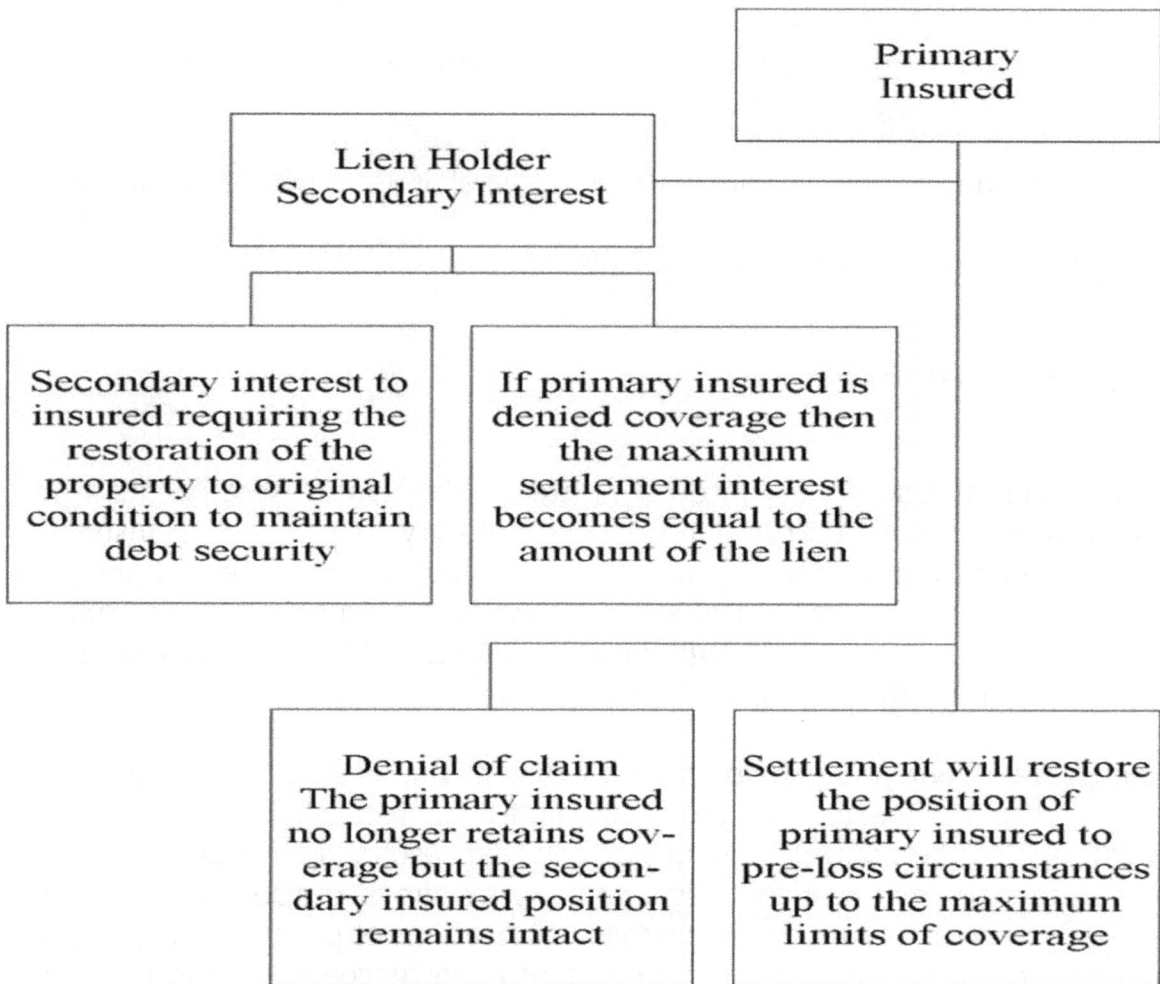

Figure 1:8   Primary and Secondary Interest

Example: An insured's claim is denied because the loss is found to be the result of an act of arson on the part of the insured.

The insured will not receive any financial or other settlement as a result of the claim.

The mortgage holder will retain coverage and will receive settlement on the claim.

The mortgage holder claims losses up to the amount of the lien held against the subject property.

The mortgage holder releases any interest in the property to the insured as a condition of settlement.

A mortgage or lien holder is typically not entitled to the maximum coverage benefits provided under the policy. The settlement due to the mortgage holder will usually be set at a maximum amount equal to the amount owed to the mortgage holder under the mortgage note or recorded lien.

If the individual named on the policy is found to be ineligible for coverage and the mortgage holder receives the total due to them under the note, the insurer will usually receive a transfer of any interest held by the mortgage holder in the property. The release of the lien or interest in the property is a condition that is required to finalize the claim settlement to the mortgage holder.

When a lien holder interest exists on the property, the lien holder has the right to be included on any loss settlement check made to the insured that apply to the dwelling secured under the lien.

What this means to you is that when a settlement check is made applicable to the dwelling, both the insured and the lien holder will be named as payees on the check. This dual endorsement ensures that the interest of the lien holder in the property is protected by enabling them to confirm that the applicable loss related repairs are made. Many lien holders will require inspections to confirm both the status and quality of any repairs being made relating to the loss. These inspections help to ensure that the dwelling is restored to the same condition as it was in prior to loss and protects the security interest of the lien holder.

The lien holder may have specific confirmation forms that must be completed before they will endorse settlement payment to the insured or to any contractors who performed services in relationship to the claim. These forms are included in a later chapter. The completion of these forms is the responsibility of those receiving payment under the claim, but you should obtain a copy of the completed forms for your claim file. Retaining a copy of all applicable release forms ensures that your company is protected against any future questions or issues that may arise regarding the claim settlement.

Other insurable interest may exist and it is important that you confirm all entries on the policy regarding potential interest in the claim. Each potential interested party will have different rights under the policy. If you become aware of additional insured's or other interested parties, you must review the policy inclusions to determine the exact claims handling processes you must follow to ensure that all interested parties receive fair settlement under the claim.

LOSS EVENT DETAILS

Summary: *Claimant insured states that hot water tank failed*
Sub? Y

Details: *Insured called to report that after his wife turned the dishwasher, the water heater (located in the basement) apparently failed, draining all of the water out of the tank. The tank subsequently overheated and caught a basket of clothing on a nearby laundry table on fire.*

Police/Fire: Any City Fire Department   *Policy:*   *HO Broad Cover*

Figure 1:9 Initial Loss Report Event Information

The individual making the loss report will describe the loss, the events leading to the loss, and verify any other parties who are able to substantiate the loss specifics.

These details will be verified during the initial conversation and interview that you will hold with the insured. It is important that you correlate this initial report with the future statements of the insured. Any discrepancies that you note between the

- initial report statement

- later statements by the insured

- witness statements

- reports of legal authorities

should be clarified before you proceed with the adjusting processes. If it is found that the insured's statements conflict with physical findings, authority reports, witness statements or their own statements regarding the loss, this initial report may be used to substantiate the position of the insurer regarding the insured contradictions in a fraud investigation.

The individual who takes the initial claim report will ask the insured questions regarding any authority that may have a report regarding the claim. You will wish to obtain copies of any reports completed by the fire department called to the scene, ambulance crews who provided assistance relating to the loss, utility company representatives called to the scene, any police who attended to loss matters and any other authority that may have reports relating to the cause of loss, loss events,

CLAIM CATEGORIES AND COVERAGE

The policy will detail the effective date and time of coverage as well as the types of coverage that are in place.

Dwelling	*$ 191,000*
Other Structures	*$ 19,100*
Personal Property	*$ 98,250*
Loss of Use	*Loss sustained not to exceed 12 consecutive months*

Figure 1:10 Initial Loss Report Coverage Data

Real property will be categorized under DWELLING and OTHER STRUCTURE coverage while personal property is covered separately under the category of PERSONAL PROPERTY.

It is important that you learn to distinguish between real and personal property and gain an understanding of the specific policy requirements and coverage methodology for each category.

Each coverage element will require you to perform different functions for the insured and handle settlement using specific methodology.

Some elements of the coverage may require the payment of a deductible while others may be paid in full to the insured from the first dollar.

OTHER COVERAGE

The insured may hold more than one policy that will apply to the loss. It is important that you verify the existence of any other coverage pertaining to any element of the claim.

Example: The property owner holds a policy that applies to real and personal property and the tenant of the property holds a policy that applies to their personal property.

If the property owner and the tenant hold separate policies that may apply to the loss, it is important that you review the inclusions and exclusions of both policies. You must also work with the insured and the other party to separate the claim elements so that the proper policy coverage is applied. This assists in protecting your company against a potential overpayment on the claim.

Other coverage may apply for other reasons beyond coverage for different interested parties or coverage that applies to different claim elements.

Example: The insured may have obtained new coverage and not cancelled the old coverage on the property.

The mortgage company and the insured may both have placed coverage on the property resulting in a doubling of coverage.

Regardless of the cause, when more than one protective policy exists on the property you should conduct additional research into the status, reason for existence, and potential overlaps of coverage.

When duplicate or overlapping coverage exists, it is essential that you perform additional research to determine if the coverage is a result of common error, inadvertent overlap, or an indicator of potential fraud.

If you discovers other insurance that may apply to the claim, both policies must be examined to determine the methods of claims settlement that will apply.

The policy of the insurer for whom you are completing adjusting functions will often detail the handling of a claim when other insurance or overlapping coverage applies to the claim. If you discover overlapping coverage or other insurance coverage pertaining to a claim, you should consult with the claims management supervisor for direction on the handling of the settlement processes and to gain assistance in navigating the application of coverage, pro-rata of coverage, and any investigations resulting from the multiple coverage's.

DWELLING COVERAGE

Our Promise

We will pay for loss to:

1. **Your** dwelling at the residence premises shown on the **Declarations**. Dwelling includes attached structures, and building equipment and fixtures servicing the premises.

---

2. Construction material at the **residence premises** for use in connection with **your** dwelling.

This coverage does not apply to land or water, including natural water, above or below the surface of the ground.

Figure 1:11 Coverage Extraction Sample - Dwelling Coverage

The policy declaration page will provide the name of the dwelling or property covered under the policy. Most standard homeowner's coverage applies only to the dwelling named on the policy declarations page.

You should compare the loss report to the property address detailed on the policy declaration page to confirm that the loss applies to the designated dwelling.

Dwelling coverage would apply to the primary structure as well as to any item physically attached to the property.

Example: Built in shelves are considered to be part of the dwelling and are covered under the dwelling portion of the claim.

Freestanding shelves are considered movables and are therefore covered under the personal property portion of the claim.

Example: An attached garage built at the residence becomes a permanent part of the structure. The garage is then covered under the dwelling portion of the claim.

A detached garage is considered other structures and may be covered under a different category in the claim if other structure coverage exists.

```
                        ┌─────────────────┐
                        │   FIRE LOSS     │
                        │                 │
                        │   Allocation    │
                        └────────┬────────┘
        ┌──────────────┬─────────┴─────────┬──────────────┐
┌───────────────┐ ┌──────────────┐ ┌──────────────┐ ┌──────────────┐
│ Free Standing │ │Built-In Shelving│ │   Attached   │ │ Storage Shed │
│   Cabinet     │ │              │ │    Garage    │ │              │
└───────┬───────┘ └──────┬───────┘ └──────┬───────┘ └──────┬───────┘
┌───────────────┐ ┌──────────────┐ ┌──────────────┐ ┌──────────────┐
│   Personal    │ │   Dwelling   │ │   Dwelling   │ │Other Structure│
│   Property    │ │              │ │              │ │              │
└───────────────┘ └──────────────┘ └──────────────┘ └──────────────┘
```

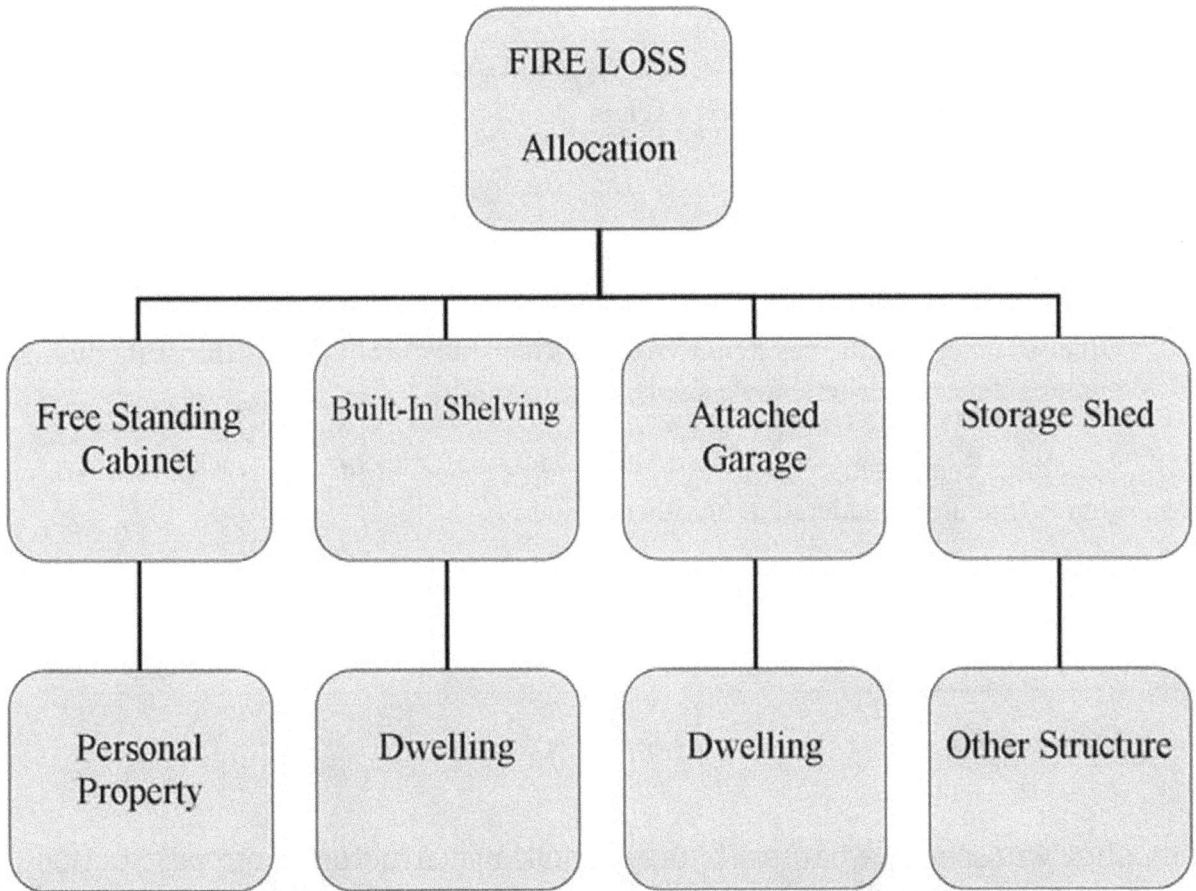

Figure 1:12 Fire Loss Coverage Allocation

It is essential that you become adept at the categorization of damaged property. Each coverage type will carry maximum limitations, special exclusions, and other variables that you must apply during the adjusting process. Properly allocating each item to the correct coverage category helps to maximize the adjusting process and ensures that the claim settlement is fair for both the insured and the insurer.

OTHER STRUCTURES COVERAGE

Our Promise

We will pay for loss to:

1.   Other structures at the **residence premises** separated from the dwelling, including garages, fences, shelters, tools sheds, or carports.

Structures connected to the dwelling by only a fence, utility line, or similar connection are considered to be other structures.

2.   Construction material at the **residence premises** for use in connection with **your** other structures.

Figure 1:13 Coverage Extraction Sample - Other Structures and Materials

The policy will specify whether fixtures, additional structures, or construction materials at the claim location will be covered under the policy.

To be covered under the other structure portion of the policy, the structure must be separated from the dwelling. Any item that is physically attached to the dwelling will be subject to the dwelling coverage parameters.

It is important that you review the specific coverage limitations applicable to other structures with the insured. The coverage amounts provided under each category may effect the settlement of the claim, especially when you are adjusting a larger loss event.

Maximum coverage limitations for other structures are often limited to 10% of the overall dwelling coverage amount.

If the loss involves multiple elements that fall under the other structure category such as a fence, a shed, and a detached garage, the damages may exceed the maximum coverage amount provided to the insured.

Example:	Loss Category	Loss Amount	Coverage Limit
	Dwelling Damage	$22,500	$185,000
	Fence Damage	$ 1,250	$ 18,500
	Storage Shed Damage	$ 7,800	$ 17,250
	Detached Garage Damage	$27,800	$ 10,550

The example illustrates a loss suffered primarily to other structures with only moderate loss to the primary dwelling. Such as a loss claim that might be brought when a fire begins in the detached garage and spreads to other elements of the property.

The total coverage for physical structures under the policy is $203,500.

The total damage to the structures equals $59,350.

The insured might assume that they will receive a full loss settlement minus any applicable deductibles because the total coverage amount exceeds the total insurance amounts provided under the policy.

Categorization of coverage will enable the insured to receive only $48,800 instead of $59,350 because the portion of the damages affecting other structures exceeds the maximum coverage available under the other structures category.

 It is important that you detail the coverage elements and method of application of coverage during the initial interview with the insured so that they have an adequate understanding of the application of the coverage to their claim. This helps to set the insured's settlement expectations to correlate to the coverage available under the policy.

FIXTURES AND PERSONAL PROPERTY

A fixture is any item that is permanently attached to a structure in a manner that enables it to become a part of the structure.

Personal property can become a fixture if it is attached or modified in such a way that it becomes a permanent part of that property.

It is important that you learn to differentiate between personal property and those items that are deemed fixtures.

The coverage provided under the policy for these classifications will be separated. Maximum coverage limitations will apply to the replacement or repair of each classification of property. If you improperly assign a particular item to the personal property classification and the maximum coverage limitations of the personal property coverage is exceeded, the homeowner may not receive full payment for the claim.

Four standards can be applied when determining if an item is considered a fixture.

- the intention of the parties in the transaction

- an agreement between the parties in the transaction concerning the status of the particular item in question

- the manner in which the item is attached to the real property

- the item itself and its adaptation to the real estate

Most standards that enable the categorization of an item as a fixture or personal property relate to the status of an item at the time that the real estate transfer occurred.

When the adjustment process indicates that the settlement of a claim may exceed the maximum coverage limits of a category, you might need to conduct additional research to make a category determination. Some items that are questionable fixtures may be designated as a fixture within the original sales agreement used at the time the insured purchased the property. You may be able to review the original sales agreement to gain additional supporting documentation pertaining to the categorization of a designated item. If the sales agreement is not available for review, you must apply point three and point four to assist you in making the determination.

If you are unable to reach a categorization agreement with the insured by reviewing the manner of attachment and the adaptation of the item to the real estate, you will need to refer the final categorization decision to a claim supervisor.

We do not pay for loss to structures:

1. used in whole or in part for **business** purposes (except rental or holding for rental of structures used for private garage purposes); or

2. used to store **business** property. However, if the business property is solely owned by **anyone we protect**, we do provide coverage for the structure. The **business** property may not include gaseous or liquid fuel,

    unless the fuel is in a fuel tank that is permanently installed in a vehicle or craft which is parked or stored in the structure.

Figure 1:14 Coverage Extraction Sample – Business Property

Within the category of fixtures is secondary category known as trade fixtures. At times, the claimant may conduct all or part of their business operations from their home. When you note a specific item that is appears to be a business operations item, you should confirm whether the business goods or equipment is covered under the policy.

The declarations page will indicate whether the claimant notified the agent of the existence of the business operations at the time of the application. The policy wording will further define the coverage in place regarding business equipment or trade fixtures.

> When an item is installed in the property for use for the business rather than installed in the property as an improvement to the building, it might be considered as personal property rather than as a fixture covered under the dwelling coverage. Theoretically, items installed in the property for

use as a part of the business operations will be removed if the business should cease or be relocated to another location.

Items that are installed in the property for use in a business may also be counted as part of the business worth. Any item that is considered part of the worth of the business cannot then be counted as part of the value of the dwelling and would not be covered under the category of dwelling coverage.

It is important that you clarify the use of any item before you categorize the item as either a fixture or personal property matter. It is possible that the insurer for whom you are completing adjusting functions provided both the personal and the business policy to the insured. When both policy issuances are from the same insured, you may be required to provide adjusting functions for both the business and personal claim. The initial loss report will often not reflect a secondary policy held by the insured for business coverage.

If the insured operates a business or conducts business activity at the loss location, you must verify if the insurer for whom you are completing adjusting activity provides coverage for the business property loss.

The insured may hold a policy issued by another insurer that provides coverage for business property at the loss location. If a secondary policy exists, an adjuster from the other insurer will often complete adjusting activity in tandem with your processes. You must work with this secondary adjuster to define the damages that will be assessed to the second coverage.

The insured may not have any coverage relating to the business functions conducted at the residence. If no coverage exists relating to business operations conducted on the premises, you should refer the matter to a senior claims supervisor for a determination of coverage to the structure. Business goods and trade fixtures will typically be excluded from the claim. The coverage provided under the dwelling or other structure portion of the policy may be denied if the business operations relate to another company. If the business is owned solely by the insured, coverage may still be provided for damages to the structure resulting from the loss event.

PERSONAL PROPERTY COVERAGE

Our Promise

We will pay for loss to:

1.   Personal property owned or used by anyone we protect anywhere in the world.

Figure 1:15 Coverage Extraction Sample – Personal Property

Coverage may be in place for the personal property of an insured when they are not at the residence listed on the policy declarations. If coverage exists for personal property when the insured is away from the residence, you may be called upon to adjust the claim.

It is important that you review the policy conditions to determine the existence or lack of coverage relating to personal property when it is not at the residence.

Example: An insured is traveling to another state and a laptop computer is damaged during travel.

If the insured has a clause within the policy terms that provides for coverage of personal property while traveling, the loss may be eligible for coverage, however, the cause of the loss will then become an issue.

You must confirm that the damage to the laptop is a result of a *'peril we insure against'.*

When a claim is made for an item that was damaged or stolen while away from the policy residence, you should review the policy coverage's and exclusions to determine

- The coverage or exclusion status of the specific item

- Location coverage or exclusion

- That the claim cause is for a *Peril We Insure Against*

When you are completing adjusting functions for an item of personal property damaged when the insured was away from the dwelling location, you should obtain all reports relating to the claim.

Example: A laptop is stolen from the insured while the insured was at a business conference.

A report is filed with the conference hosts.

A report is filed with the police department providing services at the location of the conference.

The inclusions and statements within these reports will provide a base for the claim file and your investigation activity.

Any time a report relating to a claim you are adjusting is available from an independent third party, you should obtain a copy for review. These reports can provide you with critical claim information, including indicators of possible fraud or other information that may lead to a denial of the claim.

---

2.   At **your** option, personal property owned by others while the property is on **your residence premises**.

3.   At your option, personal property of:

a.   guests and **residence employees** while the property is in a residence occupied by **anyone we protect**.

b.   **residence employees**, away from the **residence premises** while actually engaged in the service of **anyone we protect**.

4.   At **your** option, building, additions, alterations, fixtures, improvements, or installations made, or acquired at your expense, by **you** for an amount not exceeding 10% of the amount of insurance under this coverage. Payment will not increase the applicable amount of insurance under this policy.

Figure 1:16 Coverage Extraction Sample - Personal Property of Others

When a loss occurs, the insured has the option of applying the coverage that they hold to cover a loss to the personal property of others. This same loss cause and coverage limitations apply to the property of other individuals in the same manner it applies to the personal property of the insured.

It is important that you clarify the maximum limitations that the policy owner is entitled to with regard to personal property. The policy declarations page will specify the exact amount of coverage that will be provided to the claimant for each coverage category. You should also define the deductible amount applicable to the claim for the insured. Ensuring that the insured has a well-defined understanding of the policy application with regard to personal property claims enables them to make an informed decision with regard to the claim coverage allocations.

Example:		
	Maximum Personal Property Coverage	$98,250
	Deductible	$ 1,000
	Insured Personal Property Damages	$87,550
	Remaining Coverage Amount	$ 9,700
	Other Individuals Personal Property Damages	$11,850
	Coverage Deficit	$ 2,150

The policyholder will have certain options written into the policy that provide for extended coverage for certain specific events. One such parameter is the coverage of personal property belonging to other parties. If the policyholder chooses to make personal property of other individuals a part of the claim, the amount of this coverage will become a part of the maximum limitations of the policy. Payment of these items under the policy coverage may limit the amount of personal property payment the policyholder may obtain on their own behalf.

It is important that you review both the declarations page of the policy and special limitations with regard to personal property before continuing with the claims process involving personal property.

The policy will detail

- Specific types of personal property covered under the policy or excluded by the policy

- Ownership requirements of the personal property that will be covered under the policy

- Details pertaining to the perils against which personal property will be covered

- Maximum dollar figure limitations for specific types of personal property

> Example: $250 Animals, birds and fish
>
> $250 Money, traveler's checks, or stored value cards

- Maximum dollar figure for all personal property coverage

- Whether a rider exists that provides for replacement cost value of personal property

The policy will detail the category and specifics of personal property that will be covered under the claim as well as the limitations in coverage.

---

5.   Cemetery property, including monuments, headstones, grave markers, and urns.

6.   Animals, birds, and fish, but only while on the **residence premises**, for the following perils to the extent covered under *Perils We Insure Against; Fire or Lightening, Windstorm or Hail, Explosion, Sonic Boom, Riot or Civil Commotion, Aircraft, Vehicles, Smoke and Vandalism or Malicious Mischief.*

7.   Electronic apparatus and equipment:

---

a.   while in or upon a motor vehicle or other motorized land conveyance; and

b.   if the electronic apparatus is equipped to be operated by power from the electrical system of the vehicle or conveyance while retaining its capability of being operated by other sources of power.

Electronic apparatus includes cellular phones, fax machines, radios, tape and disc players, and similar equipment or devices for the recording, reproduction, receiving or transmitting of sound and pictures. Electronic apparatus also includes accessories used in conjunction with such apparatus; including antennas, tapes, wires, records, discs or other media.

Figure 1:17 Coverage Extraction Sample – Example Personal Property Type Details

The policy will stipulate additional coverage's or exclusions that may apply to the loss. These additional options may be subject to specific amount of coverage limitations and damage cause parameters.

You should review all of the stipulations within the policy prior to the first meeting with the insured and then again after you have made a claim assessment to ensure that you have the information available to make the applicable adjusting determinations.

We do not pay for loss to:

1.   Land motor vehicles and parts.

    a.   We do cover vehicles not subject to motor vehicle registration which are

        1.   Designed to assist the handicapped; or

        2.   Used solely to service the residence premises.

2.   **Aircraft** and parts

3. Electronic apparatus and equipment, which is solely powered for the electrical system of motor vehicles or any other motorized land conveyances.

4. Property rented or held for rental to others away from the **residence premises.**

5. Property of roomers, boarders or tenants not related to **anyone we protect**.

6. Any of the following:

   a. Books of account, drawings, or other paper records containing **business** data; or

   b. Electronic data processing tapes, wires, records, discs, or other software media containing **business** data. This includes **business** data stored in computers and related equipment.

   However, we do cover the cost of unexposed or blank records or media.

7. Radar Detectors.

8. Property specifically insured by this or any other insurance.

9. Except as provided under *Special Limits – Personal Property*, property, pertaining to a **business** conducted away from the **residence premi**ses unless at the time of loss such property is on the **residence premises**. However, we do not cover such property on the **residence premises** while it is stored, held as samples, or held for sale or delivery after sale.

10. Land or water, including natural water, above or below the surface of the ground.

Figure 1:18 Coverage Extraction Sample - Property Exclusion Details

You will want to confirm

- the location of the claim incident

- coverage details for the specified loss item

- that the loss is covered under the policy and not subject to exclusion limitations

Each policy will contain specific parameters regarding those items that are considered personal property. It is important that you review the policy wording to determine

- the potential coverage or exclusion of each item of personal property

- limitations that may apply to the specific item(s) of personal property

- maximum coverage provided for all personal property

- whether coverage is at the discretion of the policy holder or an automatic coverage event

- personal property riders applicable to the claim such as the replacement cost rider

Each factor relating to the settlement of personal property should be explained to the insured during the initial meeting. You may need to revisit certain exclusions or coverage stipulations when the insured completes the personal property inventory form. It is important that you set the expectations of the insured early in the adjusting process to maximize the satisfaction of the insured with the claim settlement.

LOSS OF USE

OUR PROMISE

If an insured property loss makes **your residence premises** uninhabitable, we will pay all reasonable additional living expenses while you and members of your household reside elsewhere.

Payment shall be for the shortest time required to repair or replace the premises or, if you choose, for you to permanently relocate.

These payments will not exceed a 12 month period.

We will also pay for **your** loss of normal rents resulting from the loss, less charges and expenses, which do not continue while the rented part of the residence premises is uninhabitable. We will pay this loss of normal rents only until the rented part is habitable.

If a loss forma peril covered under *Perils We Insure Against* occurs at a neighboring premises, we will pay for additional living expenses and loss of normal rents for up to two weeks should civil authorities prohibit you from occupying **your** premises.

These periods of time are not limited by the expiration of this policy.

No deductible applies to this coverage.

We will not pay for loss or expense due to the cancellation of any lease or agreement.

This coverage also applies to a loss at a covered secondary location.

Figure 1:19 Coverage Extraction Sample – Loss of Use

Loss of use allows the insured and other property occupants to offset the costs of temporary housing and increased living expenses that occur as a result of a loss.

If a covered loss occurs that makes the residence premises uninhabitable, the company will pay the living expenses that are incurred beyond the regular expenses of the insured and the household members of the insured.

This coverage enables the insured and those who were regular inhabitants of the loss dwelling to obtain temporary housing, replacement personal property, and offset food, travel, and other expenses that are incurred as a result of the claim. This coverage often stipulates that only those expenses that exceed those normally incurred by the insured will be paid. The policy will stipulate what items will fall under the loss of use category and what other items may be allocated under other coverage.

Example: Hotel Expenses   Loss of Use

Short Term Rental Costs	Loss of Use
Excess Travel Costs	Loss of Use
Replacement Personal Property	Personal Property Coverage

The insured should be cautioned regarding the language of the loss of use coverage. Most policies provide coverage for those expenses incurred in EXCESS of the regular expenses of the insured. This means that only those items that exceed the regular living expenses of the insured will be paid under the claim.

Example: The electric company stops power services to the property following a loss by fire.

The insured is no longer incurring electric service charges because the service has been stopped.

The insured begins electric service at the temporary housing location chosen while the loss residence is being restored to its original condition.

The electric bill incurred at the new residence will be the responsibility of the insured up to the regular or average amount of the electrical service that was obtained at the loss residence.

Any electric service charges in excess of the average billing at the loss residence will be offset by the loss of use coverage.

Example: The average electric bill at the loss residence is $48/month.

The temporary residence is heated by electric service.

The average electric bill at the temporary residence is $225 / month.

The insured pays $48 / month for the temporary residence electric service.

The insurer pays $177 / month for the temporary residence electric service under the loss of use coverage.

Each loss of use scenario will differ. It is important that you obtain copies of average billings at the loss dwelling or a payment history for each applicable expense so that you may adjust the coverage settlement accordingly.

When utility services are halted as part of the property protection activity following a loss event, service fees may be applied to the insured's billing. When the necessary repairs have been completed at the dwelling, the utility company will often assess service charges to inspect the repairs and restore the applicable services. Inspection and restoration of service fees are typically allocated under the dwelling coverage. You may need to address the allocation of service fees with a claim supervisor the claim settlement reaches or exceeds the maximum limits of the policy.

A specific time allocation for the loss of use coverage will be set forth within the policy. The time allocation for loss of use coverage may be amended on the policy declaration page or through a policy rider. A common term of loss of use coverage is 12-months from the date of the occurrence of the peril that caused the loss.

SPECIAL COVERAGE
OTHER DWELLINGS

Coverage may be provided to the insured for temporary loss of use resulting from a peril at a neighboring property.

Example: A neighboring property is a business premises.

Hazardous chemicals are used to conduct the business.

A chemical spill occurs at the neighboring business property.

Authorities order the insured to evacuate their dwelling until the chemical hazards can be remedied.

Temporary coverage is provided to the insured under the loss of use coverage of the policy.

NOTE: The insurer will typically attempt to regain the expenses resulting from the peril at the neighboring property.

NOTE: The ability to gain coverage for an event at a neighboring dwelling will often be subject to the same *Perils We Insure Against* stipulations as the primary dwelling coverage.

Special coverage designators, peril stipulations, and time limitations will usually be incorporated to refine the coverage that will be provided to the insured as a result of a peril at a neighboring property. You should define special coverage considerations for the insured so that they have correct expectations regarding any incurred expenses.

SPECIAL COVERAGE
LOSS OF RENT OR INCOME

The loss of use terminology will detail the handling of any lost income suffered by the insured as a result of the loss. Rental income may be offset under the loss of use coverage, but cancelled leases are usually not offset by the insurer.

The rental leases or proof of business licenses and income will be necessary to assist you with the settlement of a claim for loss of income. You will need to verify the inclusions of these documents before you can proceed with the settlement calculations for lost income resulting from the peril.

SPECIAL EXCEPTION
INSURED ACTION - RELOCATION

The policy will stipulate the basis for the loss of use payments. The stipulations pertaining to loss of use will often include a clause that if the insured chooses to relocate to a new dwelling permanently, the insurer is not required to continue to make loss of use payments under the policy terms.

At times, an insured may choose to rent a premises or purchase a new home rather than stay in temporary housing during the repair or replacement process. If the insured chooses to obtain a permanent residence rather than make use of temporary housing, the insurer is no longer obligated to make loss of use payments under the policy.

Adjusters will often assist homeowners to obtain temporary housing during the repair or replacement process. It is important that you define the limitations of the loss of use coverage before the insured makes any commitments or decisions pertaining to temporary housing.

Many areas have service companies who assist in locating short-term lease agreements, obtaining temporary furnishings, and addressing other issues that relate to temporary housing. It is important that you complete a scope of work and scope timeline before your insured commits to a specific lease or longer-term temporary housing arrangement.

Other applications of the loss of use clause might include the payment of rents lost due to the peril, temporary relocation of those who reside at a neighboring premise if the premises are damages because of the peril occurrence at the insured property or a loss that occurs at a secondary location covered under the policy.

You should review the loss of use terms to determine the status of potential coverage if an unusual loss of use question arises during the adjusting processes.

The policy will detail if the loss of use coverage is subject to a specific deductible or if all loss of use expenses are covered from the first dollar.

Upon review of the preliminary loss report and the basic policy coverage's and exclusions, you will meet with the insured to gain a better understanding of the cause of the loss, the extent of the damages and other details.

CHAPTER

2

Insured Interview

*You must meet with the insured to define
the claim process, loss coverage, and begin
the adjusting functions. This interview will
provide essential details that will assist you
in completing the tasks that lead to fair
claim settlement.*

After you have completed your review of the loss report and insurance policy,
you will schedule an appointment to meet with the insured. This meeting should
take place at the loss location so that both parties are able to review the
elements of the claim and begin planning a settlement strategy. You should plan
on this initial interview lasting for an extended period. This interview is your
opportunity to

- speak with the insured

- form the relationship that will set the tone for the claim process

- define the coverage available to the insured

- detail the claims process for your insured

- begin the process of evaluating the costs and extent of the claim

- answer any questions that the insured has regarding claim settlement

It is important that you remember that while the claims process is commonplace to you, this loss is a major event in the life of your insured. Many individuals for whom you will perform claims adjusting activities will not have experience with the claim process. During this meeting, you must help to put the insured at ease, define the parameters of the policy coverage, and outline the processes that will occur during the handling of the claim. You must ensure that your practices with the insured are compassionate, fair, and reassuring. The insured has chosen to entrust the company you represent with the most valuable tangible items in their life and it is critical that you maintain the professionalism that they expect to receive from the insurance company.

A critical element in the career of an insurance claims adjuster is the ability to blend the compassion necessary to assist the insured in feeling confident in your company with the honesty that ensures that there is no confusion regarding policy coverage, exclusions, limitations, and claims handling processes.

During the initial interview with the insured you must

1. Define the coverage of the policy

2. Elaborate on any specific exclusions and limitations

3. Explain the adjustment process

   a. Property inspection

   b. Claim evaluation

   c. Costs appraisal

   d. Cause investigations

   e. Property restoration or replacement

   f. Payments

4. Define the steps that the policyholder must take to protect the property against further loss

5. Assist the policyholder in retaining the services of a restoration company when necessary

6. Ensure that the policyholder has adequate temporary housing when necessary

7. Provide advance payments to offset immediate claim related expenses

8. Explain expense receipt criteria and remittal processes to the policy holder

9. Provide blank inventory forms to the policyholder so that they may begin creating an inventory of loss items

10. Obtain a non-waiver release from the policy holder

11. Gain a statement from the insured relating to the claim

    a. confirm the full name of the policy holder and other interested parties

    b. gain details pertaining to any other insurance coverage that might exist

    c. obtain specifics information regarding the cause of the loss

    d. define the insured's theories regarding the cause of the peril, extent of the loss and damages that will be included in the claim

12. Address any questions that the policy holder has regarding the coverage, claim, processes or other matters

13. Conclude the initial meeting

ADVANCE PAYMENTS

When you meet with the insured, you will often provide the insured with an advance payment to cover immediate needs resulting from the loss. These immediate needs might include the

- costs of temporary housing

- clothing and essentials until personal property can be accessed

- the cost of meals that will be obtained outside of the home until the extent of the loss damages can be assessed

- additional travel expenses incurred due to the temporary relocation of the insured

You may be required to issue additional advance payments throughout the claims process to help maintain the insured during temporary relocation. These subsequent advance payments are often remitted based upon reimbursement receipts provided to you by the insured.

The advance payments that you provide to the insured will be categorized as loss of use payments unless they relate to personal property replacements. You should define the application of these payments for the insured before they make use of the funds. This clear and early explanation of the allocation of payments helps to ensure that the settlement processes flow smoothly.

The initial payment is provided to the insured under the assumption that the claim will be covered under the policy. The purpose of these payments is to provide the insured with the funds that they require over the first days of the claim and throughout the relocation to temporary housing resulting from the claim.

When the claim is small or does not require that the insured relocate during the claims process, the insured may not need the initial advance payment.

When the claim is larger, requires that the insured and other occupants temporarily relocate or when the claim includes many essential elements of personal property, you will provide an advance payment to help the insured offset these costs.

When making an advance payment, you must ensure that you act in a way that avoids waiving the rights of the insurer with regard to the claim. The courts hold that making payment to the insured waives the rights of the insurer to certain coverage defenses. You must provide financial assistance to the insured during the first days of the claim if the insured will have to bear immediate expenses as a result of the loss. This payment will be made before you complete the investigation processes of the claim. To protect yourself and insurer, you should incorporate a non-waiver statement into the receipt for advance payments or obtain the insured's signature on a non-waiver agreement before making any advance payments. These steps help to protect the insurer against an inadvertent waiving of rights. The non-waiver wording incorporated into the receipt will define certain specific reservations and stipulations with regard to the advance payment and the rights retained by the insurer. The wording will

- state that the advance payment being provided is not a statement that the insurer is accepting the claim as valid

- define the purpose of the advance payment and state that it is not to be considered a payment under the policy for the claim
- illustrate that the payment is being made as a result of statements on the part of the insured regarding the cause of the loss and the matters of the claim

- state that the insurer has not accepted or denied the rights of the insured under the claim

- illustrate that the insurer reserves all rights under the policy and is not waiving any conditions or rights through the payment

- state that the insured promises to repay the funds being provided as advance payment if the claim is denied

- define the allocation of the payment if the claim is deemed to be valid

You should instruct the insured to maintain a record of receipts for all expenses that are considered as resulting from the loss. It is important that all expenses be documented so that the insured can obtain credit for these expenses. You will review these reports to confirm that all of the entries are valid before making any future payments.

After the initial advance payment, you will often remit future payments to help offset the costs resulting from the claim by reimbursing the insured for the costs documented by the receipts. This method of providing future payment ensures that the insured has a steady flow of cash available to cover their needs following the loss.

You should obtain the record of expenses and all of the receipts that prove these expenses from the insured each time you provide them with funds during the claims process.

Each remittal of funds to the insured should contain the non-waiver terminology to ensure that the rights of the insurer remain in effect throughout the claims process.

CHAPTER

3

Claim Management

Investigation into the cause of the claim is essential to the initial determination of coverage. Confirming the cause of the loss ensures that the claim is a result of a covered peril. Claim investigation includes the definition of damages and potential claim related costs. Proper claim investigation techniques ensure that a fair settlement is reached for both the insured and insurer.

After the initial interview, you will proceed to investigate the claim. The claim investigation portion of your adjusting function incorporates multiple functions and tasks that are critical to the fair settlement of the claim. You will

- determine the cause of the loss

- inspect the property damages

- evaluate the potential costs of the claim

- discuss all damage findings with the insured

- prepare investigation reports for the claim file

A part of your job is to determine the depth of the investigation that is necessary to handle each claim. Smaller claims that have an obvious cause and damages that are clearly defined will require less investigative activity than larger claims, claims with ambiguous causes, or claims that have the potential to include costly restoration work. The investigation portion of your duties is critical to good claims settlement processes. You will investigate to determine the

- cause of the loss

- coverage of the loss

- amount of the claim

- potential issues or problems that may arise regarding settlement

- potential indicators of fraudulent activity

You will begin the investigation process by reviewing the statements that the insured provided at the time that they initially reported the claim. These statements should be similar to those that the insured provides to you during the initial interview. It is during these discussions that discrepancies in the statements of the insured will become apparent. If a discrepancy is found within the statement of the insured, it is part of your duty to determine if these were simple misstatements or an indicator of potential insurance fraud activity.

You will expand on any questionable matters by asking elaborating questions of the insured. These questions will assist you in determining if the insured is being untruthful or if the contradictory statements are a result of confusion or claim related stress.

You will obtain statements to help substantiate the facts of the loss from any individual or legal authority who was a witness to the events surrounding the loss or immediately following the loss event. These individuals can provide information that

- confirms the statements of the insured

- defines the cause of the loss

- points to questionable matters such as the possibility of arson

You should review any reports compiled by authorities who were present in relationship to the loss, such as police, fire personnel, or utility company representatives. These reports will provide you with insight into the

- facts of the loss event

- findings of any investigations conducted by these authorities

- information relating to the legal determination of the cause of the loss

- other matters, including contradictions, that might be incorporated into the reports

If the cause of the loss is ambiguous or if you suspect that the loss might be a result of an attempted fraud or act of arson, you will

- expand the investigation

- gain additional assistance from the senior staff of your company

- take steps to protect both the insurer and insured while you complete the investigation processes

As a new insurance claims adjuster, you will refer any questionable claim matter to your senior claims supervisor. The insurer has practices in place to ensure that all questionable claims are investigated while maintaining fair settlement practices for the insured. After you become adept at basic claim adjusting practices, you may wish to expand your skill base to encompass advanced claim investigation skills. A base investigation skills set is included in the course to assist you in gaining a clearer view of the steps you should take if you suspect that the claim is an act of attempted fraud.

COVERAGE AND CAUSE

You must determine the cause of the loss and confirm that the cause is a peril covered under the policy held by the insured. The determination of the cause and coverage of a loss requires that you review

- all statements

- witness observations

- report paperwork

- policy components

- policy riders

Property insurance policies will typically come in two basic forms. One type covers only specified perils while the other covers all loss instances. The type of coverage will dictate the methods that you apply to adjusting the claim. You should review the policy components to confirm the types of loss that the insured has coverage against before beginning the adjusting processes.

DWELLING AND OTHER STRUCTURES COVERAGES

We will pay for risks of direct physical loss to property insured under the *Dwelling and Other Structures Coverage* except as excluded or limited herein.

Figure 3:1 Coverage Extraction Sample – Dwelling and Other Structure Coverage

A broad statement of coverage will typically be included within the policy wording. This statement illustrates the existence of coverage. This coverage will then be limited by the specific exclusion wording incorporated into the body of the policy.

All polices will list specific coverage exclusions or perils that the company will not provide coverage against.

- Some perils are deemed to fall within an uninsurable category.

  What this means is that items such as war or nuclear hazards are not insurable by the company.

  These types of perils fall within this category because the risk of multiple claims occurring simultaneously is very high. The likelihood of multiple claims would minimize the ability of the insurance company to provide coverage for the peril while maintaining plausible premiums.

  Some perils deemed uninsurable might still be covered if the insured purchases optional coverage for the specified peril. This coverage will require the payment of additional premiums. Coverage for additional perils will often be defined within riders to the policy.

  Example: Flood Insurance Coverage

- Some perils are deemed to fall within the category of gradual hazards.

  A gradual hazard is one that occurs over time. The loss resulting from a gradual hazard could be mitigated by the homeowner as part of the regular property maintenance requirement of homeownership.

  These gradual hazards include perils such as

  Normal wear and tear

  Settling, cracking, shrinking or expansion of structure components

  Damage by birds, rodents, insects, or other animals

These perils are all preventable or minimized with action by the insured. Damages resulting from these perils will occur over time so the resulting loss is considered to be the fault of the homeowner.

We do not pay for loss

1.   Involving collapse, other than as provided in What We Also Pay, (2) Collapse;

Figure 3:2 Extraction Sample – Loss Exclusion and Specification

At times, a specific peril may be limited within the exclusions segment of the policy but still be deemed a covered peril. If a type of peril is excluded but subject to exceptions to the exclusion, the policy will detail all instances where coverage may still be obtained by the insured. The exclusionary language will reference another area of the policy where these exceptions to the exclusion are defined.

---

2.   Caused by freezing by temperature reduction of a plumbing, heating, air conditioning, gutters and drain spouts, or fire protective system, or of a household appliance, or by discharge, leakage or overflow within a system or appliance caused by freezing, while the dwelling is vacant, unoccupied or being constructed.

There is coverage if you have used reasonable car to:

a.   maintain heat in building; or

b.   shut off water supply and drain the system or appliances of water.

Figure 3:3 Extraction Sample - Exclusion with Action Exception

Some losses that are excluded within the policy language may be subject to an exception that enables coverage if the insured takes reasonable care to limit the extent of the loss. The policy will state the exclusion and then define the specific type of coverage that may apply along with the required actions on the part of the insured to gain this exception.

Additional coverage may also be available to the insured beyond the standard policy provisions. This additional coverage will usually be offered to the insured in exchange for enhance premium payments. The determination to purchase this coverage will be based on the category of risk pertaining to certain perils and the needs of the interested parties in the transaction.

An insured that has a dwelling located in a flood plain may choose to purchase flood insurance to mitigate the risks of water damages to the dwelling. The mortgagee holding an interest in the property may require flood insurance as a stipulation before the insured can obtain loan funds relating to the property.

Enhanced or supplemental coverage may be incorporated into the body of the policy, but is more frequently detailed within riders to the original policy.

The determination of the need for additional coverage or policy riders that alter the standard policy coverage agreement is one that is made between the insured and their insurance agent or by the insurer as a result of a systematic policy change.

You will review all policy inclusions, riders, and the insured's application to confirm the specific coverage and exclusion data relating to the loss.

SPECIFIED EXCLUSIONS

Other coverage exclusions will be detailed within the policy. It is important that you review each exclusion, exception, and any potential exception requirements to ensure that you have an understanding of whether the loss cause is or is not covered under the specific policy held by the insured.

Under items 1. through 10. any ensuing loss not excluded is covered.

See *Section 1 – What We Do Not Cover – Exclusions* for additional excluded.

Figure 3:4 Extraction Sample - Coverage Unless Specifically Excluded

The policy will detail all exclusions that relate to the loss. An exclusion is any item that the insurance policy specifically will not cover or any limitation that applies to the coverage.

The exclusion section of the policy will detail those perils that are not covered under the policy.

Example: The exclusion might specifically state that the policy will not cover losses resulting from earthquakes, floods, war, or another act of god.

A common exclusion in today's insurance industry is the exclusion against coverage for mold.

4.   Caused by constant or repeated seepage or leakage of water or steam over a period of weeks, months, or years from within a plumbing, heating, air conditioning, or fire protective system, or a household appliance.

However, there is coverage if the loss is sudden and accidental.

5.   Cause by:

a.   Termite, vermin, insects, rodents, birds (except glass breakage), skunks, raccoons, spiders, or reptiles.

b.   mechanical breakdown, deterioration, wear and tear, marring, inherent vice, latent defect, tree roots, rust, smog, wet or dry rot, mold, fungus or spores;

c.   the discharge, disposal, release or escape of any solid, liquid, gaseous or thermal irritant, pollutants, or contaminant including smoke, vapors,   soot, fumes, acids, alkalis, chemicals and waste. Waste includes materials to be recycled, reconditioned or reclaimed.

d.   smoke, unless the loss is sudden and accidental. Smoke from agricultural smudging or industrial operations is not covered even if the loss is sudden and accidental.

e.   bulging, cracking, expansion, settling, or shrinking in ceilings, foundations, floors, patios, decks, pavements, roofs or walls.

If a through e cause water damage not otherwise excluded from a plumbing, heating, air conditioning, or fire protective system, household appliance, waterbed or aquarium, we cover loss caused by the water. Coverage includes the cost of tearing out and replacing any part of a building necessary to repair the system or appliance. This does not include loss to the defective system or appliance (other than a waterbed or aquarium) from which the water escaped.

Figure 3:5   Extraction Sample - Specified Exclusions

Other exclusions will relate to specific types of property that are not insured. These exclusions provide a benefit to the insured in that they are only charged premiums for coverage that best applies to the most likely perils they will encounter.

Many of the exclusions relate to items or instances that do not typically apply to a standard homeowner situation or apply to instances where the cost of coverage would be excessive compared to the likelihood of an applicable claim.

The insured may obtain coverage for an excluded item if they feel that it is applicable to their situation through the purchase of a secondary policy or through a rider to the original policy. It is important that you review any applicable riders compared to the exclusions of the policy if the claim involves a potentially excluded item.

It is important that you confirm the cause of the loss and then verify the insurability of the loss under the terms of the policy.

LIMIT EXCEPTION

One additional coverage alteration that may occur is one related to a coverage limit exception. Specific situations that exist that may enable the maximum coverage limitation to be exceeded.

Example: A loss that requires debris removal

Debris removal may include structural elements, construction materials, or personal property. The costs of debris removal will often be addressed independent of other coverage within the body of the policy

The costs to protect the property from further damage and to remove debris resulting from the claim cause are often assessed by a service company retained by the insured.

These amounts are usually covered under the dwelling limitations included in the policy. At times, the amount of coverage may be exceeded during the claim process. If the maximum coverage available under the DWELLING portion of the claim is reached or exceeded, many policies allow for an increase of coverage to cover the costs of debris removal.

This increase is typically expressed as a percentage of the stated coverage.

We will pay the expense for removal of:

1.   Debris of covered property following loss under *Perils We Insure Against.*

2.   ash, dust, or particles from Volcanic Eruption that has caused direct loss to a building or property within a building; or

3.   fallen trees which cause damage to covered property, provided the coverage is not afforded elsewhere by this policy.

If the amount of insurance applying to the loss is exhausted, we will pay up to an additional 5% of the amount of insurance applying to the damaged property for removal of debris.

We will also pay up to $1000 per occurrence with a limit of $500 per tree for the removal of fallen trees on the residence premises if loss is cause by *Windstorm or Hail.*

Figure 3:6 Extraction Sample – Expense of Removal - Debris

Example:

COVERAGE	ACTION	COST	Limitation
Dwelling	Restoration	$110,000	$112,000
Dwelling	Debris Removal	$ 5,200	$112,000

The cost of restoration work plus debris removal totals $115,200. The maximum dwelling coverage of the policy is $112,000 causing a deficit in coverage of $3,200.

If specific verbiage within the policy does not detail coverage that applies specifically to the removal of debris, the insured would be responsible for payment of the $3,200 excess.

If the policy specifies up to a 5% of dwelling coverage increase then the insured would not be liable for any of the costs because the policy would allow an additional $5,600 of coverage to offset the cost of debris removal.

---

(12) ORDINANCE OR LAW COVERAGE

If a loss by a *Peril We Insure Against* occurs to covered property, or the building containing the covered property, we will pay for the increased costs incurred due to the enforcement of any ordinance or law that is in force at the time of the loss up to 10% of the amount of insurance under *Dwelling Coverage* or $5000 or greater.

You may use this coverage for:

1. the construction, demolition, renovation or repair of the portion of the building damaged by a *Peril We Insure Against*; or

2. the demolition and reconstruction of the undamaged portion of the building because of the repair or replacement of the portion of the building damaged by a *Peril We Insure Against*; or

3. the removal or replacement of the undamaged portion of the building because of the repair or replacement of the portion of the building damaged by a *Peril We Insure Against*; or

4. the removal of debris resulting from the construction, demolition, renovation, repair or replacement of 1, 2, or 3.

Ordinance or Law Coverage does not include coverage for:

1. loss in value to any covered building due to the requirements of any ordinance or law; or

2. the cost to comply with any ordinance or law requiring the testing, monitoring, cleaning up, removing, containing, treating, detoxifying, neutralizing, responding to or assessing the effects of any solid, liquid, gaseous or thermal irritant, pollutant or contaminant in or any covered building.

Figure 3:7 Extraction Sample - Ordinance of Law

Example: Mandated code upgrades to comply with statutory regulations

Many properties, especially older ones, have elements that do not comply with the standards of current construction codes.

In most jurisdictions, the homeowner is not required to upgrade to meet current code requirements as part of the normal maintenance of homeownership.

Any construction activity is required to meet current code standards.

The repair and restoration work that results from a loss settlement will need to include work that meets the current code standards. The need to meet current code standards is typically offset by the insured during the loss settlement process. The policy will include specific coverage or exclusions relating to meeting any code requirements necessary to complete the repair and restoration work that will return the insured to the pre-loss position.

In this instance, the insured does benefit from the insurance coverage and ends the settlement process in a better position than they were in prior to the loss.

---

(16) TREES, SHRUBS, PLANTS AND LAWNS

We will pay up to an additional 5% of the amount of insurance under *Dwelling Coverage* for loss to trees, shrubs, plants and lawns at the **residence premises**.

Figure 3:8 Extraction Sample – Limit Exception

Example: Landscaping details such as trees, shrubs, plants, and lawns are not categorized under the DWELLING, OTHER STRUCTURE, or PERSONAL PROPERTY segments of the policy.

Landscape elements are not typically covered under a claim unless additional coverage details are incorporated into the policy applicable to these items. If additional coverage verbiage is included in the policy, the maximum amount of coverage is typically expressed as a percentage of another coverage.

Claim amount limitations and claim cause details will often be incorporated into the policy to define the instances where landscape elements may be covered. It is important that you review all of the additional coverage verbiage with the insured to ensure that they have an adequate understanding of the potential settlement determination on the claim.

It is important that you understand that coverage limits set forth in the policy binder may, at times, be exceeded if the correct additional coverage verbiage is included as part of the policy. You should review the entire policy to note any additional coverage or limit exceptions that may apply to the loss before meeting with the insured.

ADDITIONAL COVERAGE

The policy may incorporate additional coverage elements that are detailed separately within the primary policy or incorporated into riders of the policy.

Additional coverage may apply to the cause of loss, but more frequently apply to actions relating to the claim such as debris removal or fire department charges.

---

(6) FIRE DEPARTMENT SERVICE CHARGES

We will pay all reasonable fire department service charges to save or protect insured property. Payment is in addition to the amount of insurance applying to the loss.

No deductible applies to this coverage.

(7) FIRE EXTINGUISHER RECHARGE

We will pay all expenses incurred to recharge portable fire extinguishers after they are used to fight a fire.

No deductible applies to this coverage.

Figure 3:9 Extraction Sample - Fire Department Charges

Fire departments that serve rural areas or areas where there is a fee for service contract between the fire department and area homeowners may cause service charges to be incurred with regard to certain loss causes. The policy will specify the extent of coverage for any fire department service charges that are incurred in relationship to the loss. The policy will further detail the handling of any deductible applicable to the policy with regard to these charges.

SUPPLEMENTAL COVERAGE

Separate riders may apply to the policy that will alter or amend the coverage conditions. These riders should be reviewed in conjunction with the original policy to ensure that you have a full understanding of the limitations, exclusions, and coverage before you proceed with the adjustment processes.

At times, the insured may purchase supplemental coverage along with the standard policy. This supplemental coverage is termed a rider or additional coverage.

Common supplemental coverage riders include sewer line back up coverage or personal property replacement cost riders. It is important that you review any supplemental coverage, policy riders, and policy amendments before proceeding with the claims process.

ACTION AND PROTECTION CLAUSE

8.   by neglect of anyone we protect to use all reasonable means to protect covered property at and after the time of loss or when property is threatened by a peril covered under Perils We Insure Against.

9.   by intentional loss, meaning any loss arising from an act committed by or at the direction of **anyone we protect** with the intent to cause a loss.

Figure 3:10   Extraction Sample - Action or Inaction Exclusions

---

(6) INCREASE OF HAZARD

Unless we agree beforehand, coverage is suspended if hazard is substantially increased by any means within control or knowledge of **anyone we protect**.

Figure 3:11 Extraction Sample - Increase of Hazard Exclusion

The costs of protecting the property from further damage can often be assessed as part of the claims process. These charges will be incorporated into the claim scope that you create during the adjusting activity.

These actions are sometimes termed reasonable repairs within the wording of the policy. The insured should be instructed to make any necessary protective repairs to the property during the initial claim report and again when you contact the insured to arrange the initial interview. You should council the insured to maintain a record of all expenses incurred during the protection phase of the claim to ensure that reimbursement for the immediate expenses can be obtained from the insurer.

RESTORATION SERVICE CONTRACTOR

In many cases, a service company will be retained to assist the insured in completing the assessment of damages, opted restoration work, and disposal of damaged goods.

These service companies are professional restoration firms whose function is to complete the physical requirements of the claim and facilitate a smooth process for the insured. While these restoration companies work for the insured, given the nature of their function, much of the negotiation and work process activity of this company will be conducted with you.

At times, the insured may remit the deductible payment directly to the restoration services company. If payment in the amount of the deductible is made by the insured to the restoration company, it is important that you obtain a copy of both the contract illustrating the negotiations between the insured and the service company and the receipt for the payment in the amount of the deductible for your file records. This will assist you in rectifying the claim figures and provides a paper trail that ensures all of the financials of the claim are correctly applied.

It is important to remember that the service restoration company is contracted to work for the insured. You will have contact with the representatives of this restoration company and may negotiate with them when they are acting in the negotiations on behalf of the insured, but final work orders, payment requirements, and contractual obligations must be finalized between the insured and the restoration company.

Service contract inclusions and exclusions will vary depending on the company retained by the insured. You should familiarize yourself with the inclusions of any service contract entered into by the insured of a claim you are adjusting. An example of a general service contract is included below. You will note that many of the service inclusions of the contract mirror the required insured actions stipulated on the policy.

WORK AUTHORIZATION In order to start our emergency restoration services, you must sign the Authorization to Perform Services Form. This lets us take action immediately. We do not know your insurance coverage, therefore it is impossible for us to know exactly what your insurance will cover. It is important to understand YOU ARE FINACIALLY RESPONSIBLE FOR OUR SERVICES. Your deductible is payable to _____ before we start work. If for any reason insurance coverage cannot be verified at the time of our emergency service, an additional deposit may be required.

Date Damage Occurred: _____

Insurance Carrier: _____

Policy #: _____

Verified: _____

Deductible Amount: $_____

OUR INSURANCE is properly issued with appropriate business insurance.

REFERENCES: We would be pleased to provide references upon request.

HOW WE PROCEED:
Surveying and Pretesting – The process of surveying the job environment is an in-depth process. First, we will walk through the job with you to determine the areas that have been affected. Second, we will pretest the cleanability of surfaces as needed. Pretesting is a process designed to identify those items that will be restorable. Third, we will make a detailed scope and inventory of each affected area in your home. Finally, we will give you a summary of our findings and explain the best steps for restoration.

Extent of Cleaning – We will restore to full extent of the smoke damage. However, you and your insurance adjuster have the final say as to the extent of cleaning to be performed. Please consult with your adjuster if you have any questions. You will be responsible to pay for anything your insurance company does not pay for.

Metal Polishing – Unless conditions warrant chemical restoration, metal such as silver and brass will be cleaned and buffed only. Polishing will only be done if we are authorized both you and the adjuster.

Floor Finishing – Hard surface floors will be mop cleaned. Stripping, sealing and refinishing will only be done if conditions warrant and we are authorized by both you and the adjuster.

CUSTOMER INFORMATION – FIRE DAMAGE

Clean/Prep for Paint – Wall and ceiling surfaces which are heavily smoked and will not clean completely, will be cleaned so that sealor paint will adhere. These surfaces may clean up better with additional work. However, the type of additional work is not authorized or paid for by insurance companies when painting is still required. If you request non-covered services, you will be responsible to pay for them.
anything out unless you request it.

Deodorizing – We guarantee our deodorizing to be complete provided that all sources of odor have been removed, cleaned, or sealed.

Clothing – Your insurance company may encourage you to clean any affected clothing in your home. If the damage is too heavy or if facilities are not available, we will recommend a local professional laundry and dry cleaner we use to do the work. You may use any laundry or dry cleaner that you wish, however it is important that they be familiar with smoke damage.

Ductwork – If you have forced air heat, we will inspect your system to determine if smoke has entered the ductwork. If so, we will recommend measures to remedy the situation.

WHAT IS RESTORABLE We will separate and save any items which do not clean completely. Our crews will never throw

PRE-EXISTING OR PRE-LOSS CONDITIONS During the course of cleaning, it is likely we will remove normal soil, which existed prior to your loss. We are happy to do so. If, however, the removal of pre-existing soil requires significant extra effort, our crews will be instructed to move on to the next item. Pre-existing damage will also be noted.

PERSONAL ITEMS In the course of our survey and cleaning, we will sometimes be required to open doors, cupboards, etc. to qualify and/or restore damage. If any of these areas contain personal items you would prefer to relocate before we start work, please let us know.

GUNS AND AMMUNITION Our crews are instructed NEVER to touch guns or ammunition. For this reason, we request you remove any such items from the areas we are cleaning.

JEWELRY, VALUABLES, HEIRLOOMS Please remove any valuable items from the areas we are cleaning before the job is started. List any special heirlooms or collectibles that should be given extra special or extra delicate treatment due to their value:

_____

_____

_____

OVERLOOKED ITEMS Although our supervisors inspect all work, you certainly understand that no employee is perfect. Please bring any overlooked items to the attention of the supervisor. A final inspection of the job should also be performed with the supervisor

INSURANCE ADJUSTERS OR AGENTS We are neither of the above. We cannot authorize anything to be replaced, repaired, or painted. This is entirely between you and your insurance company. Our job is to preserve and protect, stop further damage from occurring, and to restore damaged items to their prior condition when possible.

IT IS IMPORTANT TO UNDERSTAND THAT WE WORK FOR YOU, NOT THE INSURANCE COMPANY.

HEATH AND SAFETY Maintaining your personal health and safety is of great concern to us. All occupants and pets should stay away from the work areas to protect their health and safety during the work process. Material Safety Data Sheets for our products are available upon request. Please indicate if you want copies __ Yes __ No

Please note any concerns _____

_____

APPROXIMATE COMPLETION It is difficult to estimate the actual time that will be required to complete the restoration process. We estimate approximately _____ days _____ weeks

COMMENTS _____

_____

_____

I HAVE READ AND UNDERSTAND THE ABOVE STATEMENTS AND INFORMATION CONTAINED

_____

One of the first billings that you may receive relating to a retained restoration company is the bill for the necessary repairs to secure the property against further damage. The service company will also often complete the emergency removal of personal property on behalf of the insured. These functions fall within the required actions on the part of the insured and assist to minimize the final amount of the loss.

Billings may be provided to the insured for remittal to your office or sent directly to your attention from the service company. It is important to review the contract between the insured and the restoration company regarding the remittal of payments for services rendered. The service contract should be compared to the specific verbiage of the insurance policy and insurer standard practices manuals. If a discrepancy between the coverage provided under the policy and the activity completed by the service company, you must notify the insured so that they may make an informed decision before finalizing any work order with the service company. The service company will typically include a clause within their contract stating that the insured is responsible for all charges incurred. If coverage is denied or an action taken by the service company is not covered by the insurer, the insured must make the applicable payments. It is important that you provide specific coverage details to the insured before they enter into any work contract to minimize issues when the claim is settled.

When a loss payment check is provided for any repair and restoration services in relationship to the claim, these checks are typically written to the insured, other interested parties named within the policy, and the service company who has completed the applicable work. The multiple endorsement requirements created when the check includes all potential interested parties ensures that each named individual is aware of the status of the claim, has the ability to object to the dispersal of funds, and that payments for all services are provided to the correct party.

The need to include all interested parties on any settlement check will be dictated by the standard practices manual of the insurer for whom you are completing adjusting actions.

Extent of Loss

Upon ascertaining the cause of the loss, you must begin the process of assessing the extent of the loss. The extent of the loss includes all elements of the coverage provided under the policy. The ability to assess a loss, assign settlement figures to each element of the loss, and achieve fair settlement is a fundamental factor to successful property claims adjusting.

The extent of loss assessment will enable you to complete the final two steps of the investigative process

- confirming that all losses are covered under the policy

- evaluating the potential cost of the claim

You may wish to use photographs or videotape to assist you in remembering the details of the claim damages and needs. These photographic reminders will ensure that you have

- a complete assessment of the property

- a record of the extent of the damages

- proof of the personal property inclusions that might become an issue

- knowledge of special property features

- a basis for specific materials that will be needed during the repair and restoration process

The photographs or videotape may be contained to only those areas that sustained a loss in the event of a smaller claim or may need to encompass the entire structure if the claim is larger.

The combination of the property inspection and the specific provisions of the policy will assist you in making a determination as to the actual amount of recovery that will be provided under the claim.

PROPERTY DOCUMENTATION

1. You should photograph the exterior of the property from each side. This enables you to gain a comprehensive understanding of the construction, special features, and damages that will need to be addressed.

2. You should take a photograph of the roof from each side to ensure that if restoration work is necessary you have the visual documentation that you need to assess a value and determine the extent of the restoration work that will be needed.

3. If special features or visible damages exist on the exterior of the property, it is important that you obtain extra photographs of these areas so that the claim can be properly documented and managed.

You will then enter the property and take pictures following the same process.

4. Each room should be photographed in each direction.

    This enables you to obtain a photographic reminder of the

    •   construction materials

    •   layout

    •   damages

    •   personal property contained in each room

5. If special features or visible damages are noted in any room, you should take additional photographs of these items to provide yourself with a reminder of the items and with claims documentation.

It is important that you differentiate any damages that exist in the property. Damages could be pre-existing or a result of the loss cause. Those damages that are pre-existing will not be covered under the insurance claim.

You may also choose to use a video camera to document the loss. You will document the condition of the structure, including loss related damages, following the same practices and process of still photography. The benefit of videotaping the loss is the ability to add commentary relating to your observations and the entry of automatic date and time data

PROPERTY DIAGRAM

You will wish to define the property by creating a diagram that outlines the floor plan of the structure. This will assist you in recall as well as in calculating potential costs during the claims valuation process.

The floor plan should include a basic diagram of the

- Structure

- Fixtures

- Room measurements

- Damages

The diagram will typically be limited to those areas that are affected by the loss unless the claim is larger in nature, and then you may need to diagram the entire property.

DIAGRAM EXAMPLE SMALL LOSS

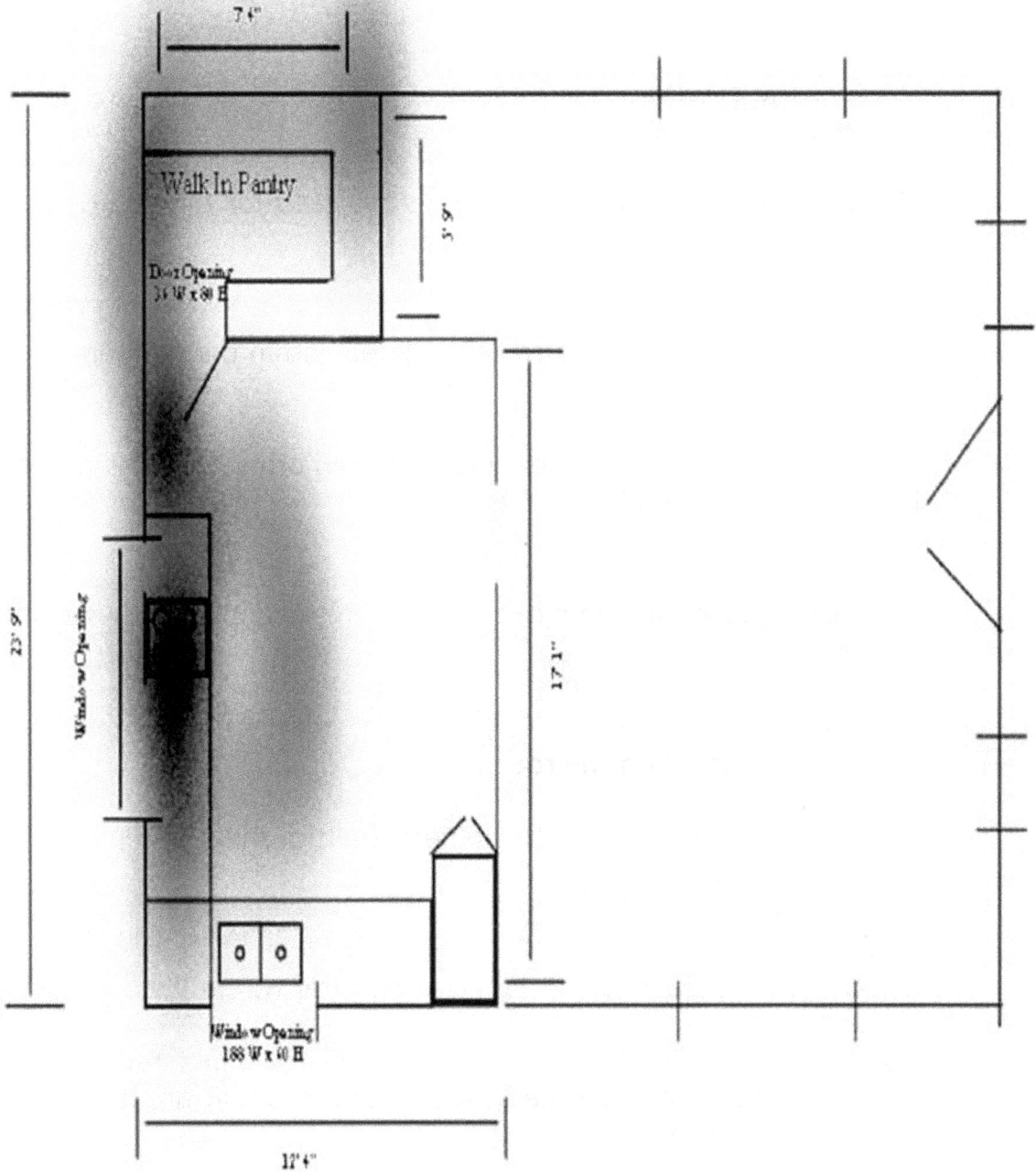

DIAGRAM EXERCISE

- Begin by creating an outline of the basic shape of the structure

- Measure the exterior areas and enter the overall dimensions on your diagram

  This initial diagram will then serve as the basis for the addition of the interior rooms

- Measure each interior area to be included within the diagram

- Place applicable walls, doors, windows, and other features of the interior in the appropriate location

- You should place the name of the room on the applicable area of the diagram

- Draw any fixtures into the room

  Common fixtures are kitchen cabinets, built in shelf systems or plumbing components.

- Define any areas of obvious damages for later reference

  The areas of the diagram that contain damages associated with the claim should be more detailed than those areas that are not affected by the loss.

DAMAGE ASSESSMENT

You will compile a damage estimate sheet that incorporates a description of the

- area of damage

- type of damage

- repairs required to mitigate the damages

- measurements of the damaged area

This assessment diagram and damage estimate will correlate to the photographs you have taken. These items will become the basis for the estimation programs you will complete when you return to the office.

Damage Assessment

Date of Loss	Date of Report

Property

Claim Number

Adjuster

Adjuster File Number

Property Floor No. _____ Base Diagram / Dimensions

Type of Building   Age

Dimensions   Total Sq Ft

No. Rooms   No. Stories

Foundation   Ext Const

Int Wall   Const

Base Diagram / Dimensions

Int Floor   Const

4:2   Example: Assessment Worksheet – Page 1

Quantity / Measurements	Detailed Description	Repair Cost	Depreciation	Total Cost

4:2   Example: Assessment Worksheet – Page 1

VALUATION

Once you have established that the loss is a result of a covered peril and inspected the property to create the preliminary assessment model, you will begin the process of determining the value of the loss. The valuation of the loss is defined as the cost of the loss to the insurer and the amount of settlement provided to the insured to bring all matters back to the prior to loss condition.

The valuation of the personal property settlement will be covered in a later chapter, for now you must begin addressing the costs of the dwelling coverage. You must address all matters relating to the loss to ensure that the claim is settled fairly for the insured but that all settlements are equitable to the insurer and follow the terms of the policy.

The specific inclusions and provisions of the policy will govern the settlement valuation process. You have reviewed the inclusions relating to the cause of loss, exclusions of loss, limitations of recovery, and the instances where these limitations may be exceeded. You will now apply all of the facets of the DWELLING coverage, OTHER STRUCTURE COVERAGE and ADDITIONAL COVERAGE to the claim. To determine the final valuation you will review

- The potential replacement cost of the property as illustrated within the maximum dwelling coverage

- The potential application of other structure coverage relating to detached property damaged by the loss

- Any limitations placed upon coverage by the wording of the policy

- Any additional coverage applications for excessive costs detailed by the wording of the policy

- Any other insurance coverage that may exist that will offset the costs of the claim

- The method of application and amount of the deductible applicable to the claim

- Any state or jurisdictional regulations that may govern the claim and supersede inclusions or exclusions detailed within the policy

- The policy and procedures manual of the insurer that has retained your adjusting services

The policy will detail the evaluation methodology to be used in relationship to the claim. These details will provide you with guidance regarding restoration, replacement, total loss, and potential areas of claim denial.

---

1.   **REPLACEMENT COSTS SETTLEMENT**
     (meaning we will not deduct for depreciation):

     a.   provided the **Declarations** shows the *Automatic No-Depreciation Settlement* applies; or

     b.   if at the time of the loss, the amount of insurance applying to the insured buildings is 80% or more of the full replacement cost of the building immediately prior to the loss; or

     c.   if the cost to repair or replace the damage to an insured building is both:

          1.   less than $2500; and
          2.   less than 5% of the amount of insurance on the building

In making a replacement cost settlement, we will pay you the cost of repair or replacement, without deduction for depreciation. Payment will not exceed the smallest of the following amounts:

     The amount of insurance applying to the building; or

     The replacement cost of that part of the building damaged for equivalent construction and use on the same premises; or

     The actual amount spent to repair or replace the damaged building

In determining 80% of the full replacement cost of the building, the value of the following will not be considered:

     a.   excavations,

---

b.   foundations below the basement floor,

c.   piers and other supports below the basement floor,

d.   if there is no basement, the value of all items below the surface of the ground inside the foundation walls.

Figure 4:1   Extraction Sample – Replacement Cost

You must make a determination of the value of the cost based upon both the repair and replace feature of the policy coverage and the total loss settlement costs of the policy. In most instances, the insurer will choose to settle the claim using whichever method of claim handling is the most cost effective.

Example: A total loss to the property would incur a maximum coverage amount of $185,000

The preliminary assessment indicates that the costs to repair and restore the structure to its original condition would incur a settlement cost of $189,000

The initial assessment of the loss total indicates that the cost to repair and restore the structure exceeds the cost to deem the structure a total loss.

You will need to complete a full scope assessment on the property to ensure that the initial cost analysis is correct and then may refer the file to a supervisor because a total loss determination would result in a total claim savings to the insurer.

In some cases, the need to declare a total loss settlement under the dwelling terms of the policy will be clear upon the initial inspection of the property. The above example illustrates a rare occurrence where the cost to repair and restore exceeds the total loss figure. A total loss determination will typically require the input of a supervisor.

You will most often handle claims that require a full scope of work assessment and the completion of restoration and repair work on the structure.

When the restoration and repair of the loss property is the most financially feasible method of settling a claim, the restoration work will typically be completed on a replacement cost basis.

The restoration work will be done to bring the property back to the condition it was in prior to the loss. This means that the cost of restoring the property may be more than the original purchase price of the supplies used in the dwelling construction.

The replacement cost settlement method requires that all restoration and repair work be completed using materials of a like kind and quality as the original materials. At times, this requirement will mean that additional work effort and cost expenditures must be put forth to maintain the satisfaction of the insured with the final work results.

Example: A portion of the siding of a vinyl sided house was damaged as a result of a covered peril.

       The original siding manufacturer no longer produces the vinyl siding.

       A perfect match for the original vinyl siding cannot be located.

       The entire property must be restored to a condition similar to it's prior to loss condition.

       All vinyl siding must be replaced to ensure that the property is restored to its original condition.

If the claim were being settled on an actual cash value basis, the insured would be entitled to the actual value or depreciated costs of similar siding in today's market. This method will take into consideration the age of the damaged siding.

If the claim is being settled on a replacement cost basis, the insured is entitled to a settlement that covers the costs for the siding in today's market without depreciation for the age of the siding.

If the claim requires that the property be restored to its original condition, the entire property must be resided to ensure that the insured attains the same position as existed prior to the loss.

It is important that you work closely with the insured to ensure that their expectations of like kind and quality match the final scope determination that you make with regard to the claim. At times, an appraisal may be required or an outside mediator called into the negotiations to ensure that both the insured and insurer are protected during the claim settlement processes.

LAND VERSUS REAL PROPERTY VALUE

Another element of the settlement process is the determination of the land upon which real property is constructed compared to the actual value of the property. In cases where the repair and restore settlement will be used, the land value will typically not become a factor in the claim. In cases where the real property will be deemed a total loss, the value of the land will become a factor in the final settlement figures.

The market value of real property includes both the value of the land and the value of all structures on the land. The property insurance policy will apply only to the structures erected on the land.

When a claim is considered a total loss, the settlement will only compensate the insured for the value of the structures on the land, not for the value of the land itself. It is considered that the land will retain its value even when a total loss occurs on the property.

To calculate the settlement amount of a total loss, you will simply take the entire market value of the property if it were offered for sale in its pre-loss condition and deduct the value of the land. The calculation results illustrate the current market value of the structure.

market value of entire property   -   market value of land   =   settlement amount

The settlement amount will be equal to that of the total market value of the property less the market value of the land only if these figures fall within the maximum dwelling coverage limitations of the policy.

VALUED POLICY LAWS

Many states have passed valued policy laws that require that the full-face amount of the policy held by the insured be paid in the event of a total loss to the property.

What this means is that it has been determined that if the insured is paying for a specified amount of coverage, the settlement of a total loss claim should equal the amount of that paid coverage. The valued policy laws require full payment regardless of the final market value determination on the property.

If the valued policy law applies to a claim you are adjusting, you must offer to settle the loss for the face amount of the policy even if it could be considered that the property was over insured and that the true market value of the property is less than the face amount of the policy.

- This valuation approach is typically applied only when the claim will be settled as a total loss rather than a partial loss.

- The valued property law applies only to dwelling and other structure claims.

- Valued property laws do not to the personal property portion of the claim.

If a valued policy law does not apply to the claim and you make a determination that settlement should be based upon a total loss, the settlement will be based on the value calculations rather than the policy limit providing that these calculations fall at or under the maximum coverage amount set forth in the policy.

Valued policy laws create a situation where you must be especially aware of the potential for fraud. Most of the inclusions of an insurance policy are written to deter fraud in that they do not create a situation where the insurer will receive a benefit from the claim. The purpose of insurance coverage is to restore the insured to the condition that they were in prior to the loss. The application of valued policy laws have the potential to improve the situation of the insured at the time that the claim is settled.

- The insurer will be careful to scrutinize the policy to ensure that the policy does not provide coverage that is in extreme excess of the value of the property insured.

- You must guard to ensure that any claim that appears to provide a financial benefit above the true value of the property to the insured is investigated properly.

Most claims are settled using a combination of cash provided to the insured and repair or restoration work paid for by the insurer. Payments for repair and restoration work are provided as payment for contractor or service company billings necessary complete the tasks included within the approved scope of work.

The policy will dictate the settlement options that may be applied to the claim and the method you will use to handle these options.

AUTOMATIC ADJUSTMENT

AUTOMATIC ADJUSTMENT OF COVERAGE AMOUNTS

This policy provides you with a guard against the effects of inflation in construction costs.

We will keep track of costs and at the next policy period we will adjust the amount of your building coverage if necessary. Adjustments in other coverages (*Other Structures Coverage and Personal Property Coverage*) will also be made proportionately. Your premium will be adjusted at each policy period to reflect any change in the amount of insurance.

During the policy period, if there is an increase in construction costs and a loss occurs, we will reflect the increase in the amount of insurance before making payment. There will be no charge for this additional coverage.

However, if for any reason other than inflation or construction costs, the amount of insurance on your home becomes inadequate, or if you made substantial improvements to your home and failed to notify us to increase the amount of your insurance, the amount of insurance shown on the **Declarations** will be the full amount.

Figure 4:2   Extraction Sample – Automatic Adjustments

Some policies will include a clause pertaining to the automatic adjustment of coverage to assist in guarding the insured against inflation and the insurer against issues that may arise when a property is underinsured. This clause provides the insurer with the right to keep track of potential increases in the replacement costs of a dwelling resulting from inflation.

The insurer will then adjust the policy limitations and coverage to reflect these increased costs and increase the premium paid by the insured accordingly. The specific time that such adjustments can occur with regard to the premium will be defined within the clause.

This clause will typically also state that if a loss occurs in the middle of a policy period and applicable adjustments to the replacement cost of a structure have not been made, settlement of the loss will be based upon these increased costs. The face value of the policy will not be used when settling the claim. This clause will also state that this increase in coverage will only apply if the cost increase is a result of inflation and not another cause.

The details of coverage will often state that the inflationary increase in coverage will only apply if the increased replacement cost is a direct result of construction cost inflation. If the increased replacement cost of the dwelling is a result of an action on the part of the insured, such as property upgrades or the erection of an addition to the property, the coverage will not automatically increase as a result.

OTHER PROVISIONS

The policy may contain additional provisions pertaining to specific types of claims, methods of determining value, or varied coverage applications that may exist with regard to the claim.

Alternate provisions or explanatory provisions are incorporated throughout the coursework. Those provisions pertaining to valuation of the claim are critical when you are conducting the claim valuation process.

Example: Pair or Set Clause

A part of a pair or set of items is damaged as a result of a covered peril

The insurer has two methods of settlement that may apply to the claim:

The insurer has the option to repair or replace the damaged portion of the pair or the set

The insurer has the option to pay the actual cash value of the damaged portion of the set

The value of a set will often total more than the value of one piece alone. If one piece of a set of items were damaged, the actual cash value for the single unit damaged would typically be less than ½ of the value of the full set.

Example: 1 chair from an antique dining set of 7 pieces is damaged beyond repair as a result of a covered peril.

The antique status makes it unlikely that a match can be found to replace the damaged item

The value of the single damaged chair is lower than 1/7 of the price of the full set

Paying the insured only the value of the damaged item would not restore the insured to the same position as existed prior to the loss

When a piece to a pair or set is damaged and a replacement for the damaged element cannot be found, you must treat the loss as a total loss to the entire set. This helps to ensure that insured is not diminished during the settlement process.

SCOPE

You will compile all of the reports you created during the investigative portion of the adjusting process into a scope estimate.

A scope is a list of the areas damaged, the damages those areas suffered, and the actions that must be taken to restore those areas to the pre-loss condition.

This scope estimate outlines the exact damages that will be addressed under the claim. The scope will illustrate the methods of repair or restoration that will be used to address each damage element. The scope should include a definition of any materials that will be used during the repair or restoration work.

This scope will serve as the financial basis for the property portion of the claim. The scope will act as an instructional guide of approved actions for any contractors retained to complete repair or restoration work at the dwelling.

You may provide a preliminary scope to the insured along with the initial reports. This enables the insured to verify their agreement with the preliminary assessment or damages to be addressed under the claim. By providing the preliminary scope to the insured early in the adjustment process, you have the opportunity to address any disputes before repair and restoration work commences.

This preliminary scope will serve as the basis for the final scope of work to be completed relating to the physical structure damages resulting from the claim. You may be required to remit a copy of the scope to any mortgagee listed on the policy or any other interested parties discovered during the investigative portion of the adjusting process.

The scope should be provided to any contractors who the insured requests to complete bids on the repair or restoration work. Any contractor who will complete work on the property will complete a bid estimate. Providing the preliminary scope of work to the contractor ensures that they create a bid that encompasses all of the work you will authorize in relationship to the claim. This helps to minimize the likelihood that the contractor will include items that are not a part of the loss claim on their bid estimate. If the contractor is unaware of the determination of damages resulting from the claim, their work estimate may incorporate costs to repair damages that were pre-existing and not a part of the loss.

The scope provides a line item comparison between your assessment, any contractor bids, and the homeowner's assessment of damages and necessary repairs.

It is important that you compile the scope estimate carefully as any discrepancies that arise during the claim may be addressed by review of this scope. You will use this scope estimate as a basis for your settlement negotiations with the homeowner and any contractors who place a bid for the repair work on the property.

Living Room		LxWxH	15'3"x12'8"x8'0"	
Missing Wall	1-5'0" x 7'0"	Opens into E	Goes to Floor	
411.37 SF Walls	193.17 SF Ceiling		604.83 SF Walls & Ceiling	
193.17 SF Floor	21.43 SY Flooring		50.83 LF Floor Perimeter	
122.00 SF Long Wall	101.33 SF Short Wall		55.83 LF Ceil. Perimeter	
Descriptions		QNTY	Remove	Replace	Total

Rewire- avg-copper	193.17 SF	0.00	1.86	359.29
R&R Phone/Low Volt-cop	50.83 LF	0.10	0.82	46.76
R&R Coaxial TV Cab	50.83 LF	0.08	0.68	38.64
R&R Outlet or Switch	5.00 EA	2.81	6.92	48.65
Detach & Reset Ceiling Fan/Light	1.00 EA	0.00	0.00	85.00
R&R Smoke Detector	1.00 EA	6.19	28.09	34.28

Figure 5:1 Sample Scope Entry - Fire Damage Living Room

The scope is a detailed analysis of all work details that are necessary to restore the structure to its original condition.

The scope will detail the damages by room. The sample scope details damages to a living room in a standard structure. This scope illustrates the restoration work required as a result of a dwelling fire. The scope includes restoration work that is necessary to remove smoke damages resulting from the fire.

L W H	The scope will first define the exact dimensions of the room. Length, Width and Height of the room will be included
Missing Wall	Any area where there is no wall will be defined. These areas will include window openings, door openings, or partial wall dividers
Total SQ FT Wall	The total square foot of all walls, less missing wall areas, will be calculated. The sum of the calculations will be entered onto the analysis portion of the scope
Total SQ FT Ceiling	The total square foot of the ceiling will be calculated and entered into the analysis portion of the scope
Total SQ FT Floor	The total square foot of the floor will be calculated and entered into the analysis portion of the scope
Portional SQ FT	Each area within the designated room will be defined by its location in the room and the square footage of that area will be included into the analysis portion of the scope

Perimeter LF   The perimeter linear foot for the areas damaged by the loss will be entered. The linear foot is the straight measurement of the area

The measurement inclusions enable the calculation of the various repair and restoration work orders that will be necessary to bring the structure back to the pre-loss condition.

Example: R&R - All Interior Walls

Primary Work Order: Remove and Replace All Interior Walls

Secondary Work Order: Seal Studs and Joists – All Interior Walls

Work Order Reason: Smoke Damage – all interior walls

When smoke damage occurs behind the walls of a structure, the repair and restore work may require the removal of all applicable walls and ceiling finish even when the surface of these materials do not have visible damage.

Removal of wall coverings enables the sealing of all wall studs to ensure that any smoke odor and potential pollutant is eradicated.

Example: Rewire – Average Residence – Copper Wiring

Work Order Reason   Rewire area necessary to restore wiring to original condition relating to R&R Interior Walls

Most insurer's require the use of a specific estimating program to ensure that the inclusions of the scope are calculated correctly, encompass all necessary components for each category of work, and include the correct baseline pricing for the region where the claim repair or restoration work is being completed.

The software available helps to ensure that the entries on the scope contain the necessary inclusions and details. These details help to ensure that all work is completed according to the policy requirements. The inclusions of the scope help to minimize the likelihood that additional work will be incorporated into the contractor's estimate and ensure that the contractor will address all necessary actions under the bid that they remit for the work.

Manual Scope Creation and Calculations

Kitchen

Floor 144 SF Wall 384 SF   Ceiling 144 SF   Floor Perim. 48 FT
                                                           Ceiling Perim. 48 FT

The first row of entries should define the measurements of the room being addressed by the scope area. Measurements are typically expressed as Square Foot, Square Yard, or Linear Foot. These measurements will act as the calculation basis for all of the work entries on the scope.

Action	Qty	Unit	Description	Cost	RC	DEP	ACV
R&R	161.28SF		Tile Floor, Vinyl High Grade	3.45	556.42	.00	556.42

Each entry on the scope should fall within a specific categorical heading. The headings included within the manual example illustrate the categorical entries you must make to quantify the inclusions and costs of the loss.

Action: all entries relating to the necessary action or function that must be complete to restore the item to its pre-loss condition will be defined. The example illustrated indicated the need to remove and replace a portion of the damaged dwelling

Quantity: most quantity entries will be expressed as a numerical figure relating to the indicated operation. Quantity relating to measurements will be extracted from the heading measurements entered on the scope. Quantity relating to a defined item such as a built-in dishwasher will be expressed as a unit. The example illustrates R&R 161.28

Unit: the unit allocation for the quantity will be included under the UNIT categorical heading. It is critical that the unit applicable to the measurement you are using as a basis for your calculation be entered correctly. The cost of a square yard of material will be much different from the cost of a square foot of material. The example illustrates 161.29 square foot of materials

Description: The description entry should encompass all of the basic details of the materials to be used in the necessary action.

Any special features applicable to the activity or materials of better or lesser than average condition must be noted within the description heading.

The description of materials or features will be used by the contractor when the bid estimate is created. If the materials or features necessary to bring the item back to the pre-loss condition are not defined on the scope, the estimate provided by the contractor may result in shortfalls, substandard restoration work, or excessive increases in the quality of items or materials used.

Cost: The cost entry will be the cost per unit for the materials.

This cost per unit will be selected from the menu of the estimating program in computer-generated scope.

The adjusting cost guide provided by the insurer will include material cost entries for many of the standard materials that are necessary for most dwelling claims.

You will

- Locate the applicable material type category

  Example: Vinyl Flooring

- Select the grade or quality comparable to the description of the material entered on the scope

  Example: High Grade

- Enter the cost per unit figure indicated within the guide

You should refer any questionable items or any items that do not have an entry with in the adjusting cost guide to a senior claims supervisor for a value determination

RC   Replacement cost entries are calculated by multiplying the unit quantity by the cost per unit figure.

Example: 161.28   x $3.45 = $556.416

Entries will be rounded to the nearest whole cent.

DEP   Most dwelling coverage will be adjusted on a replacement cost basis.

If the replacement cost settlement applies to the claim, the depreciation figure will be 0.

If the actual cash value settlement applies to the claim, you must depreciate the item being addressed on the scope row.

Example: Tile Flooring – Vinyl – Medium Grade

Cost: $468.00
Effective Life: 8   years
Age   4.5 years

Calculations: 468.00   /   8   =   58.50
              (Value)   (Life)   (Yrly Dep)

              58.50   x   4.5   =   263.25

(Yrly Dep)   (Age)   (Depreciation)

The depreciation for this item totals $263.25.

To achieve this calculation, you first obtain all of the specifics relating to the item.

- Cost
- Effective Life
- Age

You then divide the cost (value) by the effective life of the item.

468.00   /   8

The sum of your calculation is the yearly depreciation figure of the item.

=   58.50

You then multiply the yearly depreciation figure by the age of the item.

58.50   x   4.5

The sum of your calculations is the total current depreciation of the item.

=   263.25

Enter the sum of your calculations into the depreciation column on your scope.

ACV   If the actual cash value settlement applies to the claim, you must enter the actual cash value of the item into the scope. The actual cash value of an item can be calculated by subtracting the depreciation amount from the cost/value of the item.

Example: 468.00   -   263.25   =   204.75
            (Cost)   (Dep)   (ACV)

If the replacement cost settlement applies to the claim, the figure entered into the ACV field will be the same as the figure entered into the RC field, as no depreciation will apply to the calculations.

Each action required to restore the damaged area to the pre-loss condition will be entered following the same processes. The scope should be very detailed. You should create a line item detail for each action necessary to restore the property. Some entries may appear to be minute details, but it is the minute details that will ensure that the loss settlement processes are smooth and that all parties are protected.

Action	Qty	Unit	Description	Cost	RC	DEP	ACV
Room Total					2145.34	.00	2145.34

The last field entry for each room should include total room cost entries.

- The action field will contain the name of the room and the word total

- The RC field will contain the total of all replacement cost entries applicable to the room

- The depreciation field will contain the total of all depreciation calculations that apply to any element or activity within the room

- The ACV field will summarize the total of all replacement cost entries les the depreciation entries.

You should double-check all of the calculations within the scope. It is important that the dollar figures of the scope are correct. Many of the remaining actions necessary to adjust the claim and achieve settlement and closure will be based upon the entries and calculations of the scope.

If a discrepancy arises at any point during the repair and replace processes the line item entries of the scope can be used to determine the correct resolution for the discrepancy.

The contractor will prepare a bid estimate for all of the work entries on the scope. This bid estimate should be reasonable in cost. You may use an estimator program to assist in making a determination of the fairness of any bid received in relationship to the scope.

It is important that you use the insurer's handbook or recommended estimator program to complete the scope and compare contractor estimates. Estimating guides and programs will typically provide regionally appropriate cost estimates based on material availability and standard labor rates for the area where the loss occurred.

Summary for Fire			
Line Item Total			30,739.17
Total Adjustments for Base Service Charges			1,454.44
Material Sales Tax @	6.00% x	9,836.60	590.20
Cleaning Materials @	6.00% x	103.23	6.19
Subtotal			32,790.00
Overhead @	10.00% x	32,007.48	3,200.75
Profit @	10.00% x	32,007.48	3,200.75
Cleaning Sales Tax @	6.00% x	2,100.28	126.62
Grand Total			39,318.12

Figure 5:2   Sample Scope Entry - Summary for Fire

The final pages of the scope will include a summary of all of the work to be completed under the claim. This summary will include the line item total for all approved repair or restoration work determined to be a result of the loss.

Adjustments for base service charges will be included to ensure that the scope cost estimate includes all base fees, licenses and permits and other matters that will affect the total costs of the work order.

Sales tax for all materials that will be necessary to complete the scope entries will be applied based on the sales tax appropriate for the loss location.

Any standard overhead and profit figures commonly assessed by a restoration company for the type of work included within the scope will be included within the summary analysis.

These figures are dictated by

- regional practices

- industry standards

- the policy of the insurer

Standard overhead and profit inclusions may make a substantial difference to the total of the scope estimate. These amounts must be incorporated into the total settlement amount to ensure that the insurer has an adequate expectation of final costs.

The preliminary scope and final scope may be amended during the restoration processes. Any additional damages discovered during the claims process, appraisal valuation determinations, and materials costs inflation that occur prior to the completion of the restoration work might all alter the final figures of the scope. It is important that you view the scope as a final determination of work to be completed but maintain an awareness that modifications may become necessary during the claim process.

The scope estimator program that you will use for the adjusting process will prompt you to make entries of each element that leads to the generation of the final scope.

You will enter the requested data by using the diagram, assessment, and photographs obtained during your review of the property.

- Damage Area Header

- Specified Repairs

- Area Measurements

- Missing walls

- Special Features

- Construction materials

- Labor Costs

- Required Permits and Fees

- Necessary Engineering Plans

- Contractor Overhead an Profit

The estimator will assist you in generating the line item details of work that will become the final scope of work for the settlement. The estimator will provide a variety of printouts based upon your entries. You will compile these print outs into the final settlement scope.

RECAP BY CATEGORY		
O&P Items	Total Dollars	%
Acoustical Treatments	570.88	1.45
Appliances	118.08	0.30
Cabinetry	3,592.96	9.14
Cleaning	1,660.15	4.22
Concrete	115.00	0.29
Content Manipulation	205.98	0.52
General Demolition	3,950.23	10.05
Doors	302.67	0.77
Drywall	952.35	2.42
Electrical	7,848.55	19.96
Floor Covering – Carpet	365.73	0.93
Floor Covering – Wood	3,193.50	8.12
Permits and Fees	167.00	0.42
Finish Carpentry / Trimwork	273.85	0.70
Finish Hardware	74.26	0.19
Framing & Rough Carpentry	252.84	0.64
Heat, Vent & Air Conditioning	70.00	0.18
Light Fixtures	798.40	2.83
Plumbing	2,245.49	5.71

		Total Dollars	%
Painting		1,684.99	4.29
Stairs		135.00	0.34
Windows – Vinyl		453.00	1.15
Wallpaper		925.74	2.35
Subtotal		29,956.65	76.19
Basic Service Charges	@ 6.000%	1,454.44	3.70
Material Sales Tax	@ 6.000%	590.20	1.50
Cleaning Materials	@10.000%	6.19	0.02
Overhead	@10.000%	3,200.75	8.14
Profit	@10.000%	3,200.75	8.14
O&P Items Subtotal		38,408.98	97.69
Non O&P Items		Total Dollars	%
General Demolition		782.52	1.99

Figure 5:3   Scope Sample – Summary by Category

CHAPTER

6

Personal Property

A substantial portion of most property insurance claims relates to the categorization, valuation, and settlement of personal property damaged as a result of the loss. The completion of the personal property settlement will require you to work closely with the insured to ensure that all parties have a comprehensive understanding of the processes that will apply to the settlement.

Depending on the policy type and inclusions, personal property may become a large portion of the overall claim. You will provide personal property inventory forms to the insured at the time that you conduct the initial meeting. You should detail the methods that will be used to complete the forms, the timeline for remittal of the personal property inventory, and the settlement processes that will apply to the personal property damages.

You should ensure that you review the inventory forms as well as the personal property claimed as damaged to confirm both the existence of the property and the actual damage status being claimed by the insured.

The settlement basis for personal property may be actual cash value. Actual cash value compensates the insured for the current market value of any personal property damaged during the claim that is deemed to be beyond restoration or whose repair costs would exceed the actual cash value.

When ACV is the basis for payment, it is important that you view, assess, and possibly photograph the damaged personal property as many items may have intrinsic value to the insured but little or no actual cash value within the market. .

At other times, the insured may have a replacement costs rider in relationship to their personal property. The replacement cost rider can take many forms but typically allows the insured to gain the full cost of replacing any personal property item damaged during the loss event.

The specific valuation methods for determining the amount of the loss will be outlined within the policy held by the claimant.

REPLACEMENT COST

The insurance policy may contain a replacement cost clause or rider that enables the claimant to make claim for the value of an item based upon the amount that it would cost to replace it with a similar item in today's market. This clause does not depreciate the value of an item based on time, condition, or purchase period market conditions. The claimant will be reimbursed for the full amount it costs to purchase the damaged item today.

> Example: A loss caused by a kitchen fire damages a ten-year old range unit whose costs in today's market would be $468.00.
>
> Because of the age of the unit, the value within the market of a similar unit being offered for sale would fall below the purchase price.
>
> Depreciation of a unit of this age would typically limit the recovery value of the unit to $116.

A replacement cost clause within the policy would enable the claimant to purchase a comparable unit new, not of the same age, at today's market price.

This enables the claimant to obtain the full $468.00 amount on an item whose actual value is only $116.00.

We will pay no more than the actual cash value of the damage unless:

   Actual repair or replacement is complete

Figure 6:1   Extraction Sample - Replacement Cost Terms

Most replacement cost clauses contain a stipulation that the claimant will only receive the actual cash value of the damaged item until it has been repaired or replaced. Upon the repair or replacement of the damaged item, the claimant then receives the full purchase price of the unit.

- The settlement will provide payment to the insured based on the actual cash value of the item being claimed.

- The insured will purchase a replacement item of similar make and with similar features as the damaged item at the full cost in the current market.

- The insured will remit the receipt illustrating the replacement cost of the item.

- Additional settlement funds will be provided to offset the expenses incurred for the purchase of the replacement item.

LESS THAN FULL REPLACEMENT COST SETTLEMENT

If full replacement cost settlement does not apply, we will pay the larger of the following amounts, but not exceeding the amount of insurance under this policy applying to the building:

---

a.   the actual cash value of that part of the building damaged; or

b.   that proportion of the full cost to repair or replace the damage which the total amount of insurance in this policy on the damaged building bears to 80% of the replacement cost of the building.

We will not pay more than the actual cash value of the damage until the actual repair or replacement is completed.

Figure 6:2   Extraction Sample - Actual Cash Value

ACTUAL CASH VALUE

Most policies base the settlement to replace or repair items damaged under a covered loss on the actual cash value of the item. The replacement cost clause is added to some policies to modify this coverage. Actual cash value is often defined as the cost to replace a specific damaged item with deductions placed upon the replacement cost for specific depreciation in value resulting from the age and condition of the item in question.

DEPRECIATION CALCULATIONS

Depreciation may be calculated based on a straight-line method. A straight-line depreciation uses the replacement cost value and expected useful life of the item being depreciated.

Example: The replacement cost of a damaged range unit is $468.00

The expected life of the range unit is 13.5 years

The range unit is 10 years old

$468.00 /   13.5   = $ 34.68 yearly depreciation

10 years x $34.68   = $346.89 current depreciation

$468.00 - $346.89   = $121.11 depreciated value

INSURANCE ADJUSTING – REAL PROPERTY CLAIMS

(market value)(depreciation)= (depreciated value)

Straight-line depreciation may not be appropriate for all items. Straight-line depreciation assumes a specified life cycle or usefulness term of all items and then deducts a specific amount for each year of use. In some cases, this method may not be an adequate method of determining current market value for the damaged item.

Straight-line depreciation can be seen as removing a specified amount of value from an item in direct relationship to the amount of use a claimant has already received from that item.

The specified life cycle of an item will vary depending on the type of item being considered.

Example: The range unit life cycle might be considered to be 13.5 years

The life cycle of carpets installed in the home might be considered to be 10 years

The life cycle of an antique roll-top desk might be considered to be infinite

The life cycle of clothing might be considered to be 2 years

Clothing is an item that is often considered to have a much smaller life cycle than many other personal items owned by the insured.

Most insurance companies will provide you with a guide for the expected life and depreciation method to be considered for each loss item category. Computer software has been developed that enables automatic calculation of depreciation for commonly owned goods. You should complete the depreciation calculations based on the policy of the insurer that has retained your adjusting services.

Straight-line depreciation is typically factored by calculating the depreciated value of an item using the age and expected physical wear and tear obvious in relationship to the item. Physical wear and tear typically occurs regularly throughout the life cycle of an item. If the physical wear and tear of an item occurs based upon the regular and expected life cycle, then straight-line depreciation will account for the lowered value.

When the value of an item is being determined, the depreciated value can also be termed market value. Market value is the amount of money that a knowledgeable buyer would pay to obtain that item and a knowledgeable seller would accept to sell that item in the current purchase market.

At times, age may not be an adequate reflection of the actual value of some items claimed under a loss.

- Excessive wear and tear

- Replacement ability

- Obsolescence

may also affect the final claim amount in an actual cash settlement.

It is important that you review the specific depreciation guidelines set forth by the company for whom you are completing adjusting actions to determine if straight-line depreciation will apply to the claim or if other valuation factors will be considered in relationship to the items you are valuing.

EXTENT OF DAMAGES

When determining the disposition of an item claimed under the loss, a factor that must be considered is the ability to repair the damaged item. If the item can be repaired, the next considering is the costs that will be incurred during the repair process as compared to paying actual cash or replacement value of the claimed item.

When the insurer opts to repair or replace either personal or real property, it is important that the quality, materials, and other factors relating to the claimed item be considered carefully. When an insurer opts to repair a damaged item rather than provide the funds necessary to replace the item on either an actual cash or replacement cost basis, the insured must be satisfied that the condition of the repaired item is satisfactory and equal to the before loss condition. For this reason, many insurers do not choose to repair more commonly claimed item. The repair or replace option may be used when the cost to repair an item is substantially less than the costs that would be incurred to replace the claimed item.

POLICY LIMITS

The insurance policy that covers the loss will detail the specific payment limits set for the claim. These limits will typically be expressed as maximum dollar amounts that may be paid out for each of the elements covered under the policy.

The policy limits will detail the specific amount of coverage that will apply to each of the potential losses suffered under the claim. It is important that you familiarize yourself with both the limits specific to the claim you are adjusting and the categorization methods to be applied when factoring the loss.

Example: Built in shelves in a structure damaged by a fire will be applied under the dwelling coverage.

Free standing shelving units damaged by a fire will be applied under the personal property coverage.

Incorrectly allocating a claim item may result in the coverage limitations being exceeded. When a maximum coverage limit has been exceeded by the elements of a claim, any additional costs resulting from the loss will be the responsibility of the insured. If you incorrectly allocate an element of the claim and the insured suffers a financial burden as a result of the error, the insurer may become liable for damages.

Policy limits will apply in a broad manner to the coverage specifically detailed within the policy binder page. These usually include Dwelling, Other Structures, Personal Property, and Loss of Use.

In addition to the broad categorical coverage limitations, special limitations may apply to specific types of personal property. These special limits are not in addition to the coverage listed on the binder page, they are simple qualifiers for the amount of coverage that will be provided for each sub-classification.

SPECIAL LIMITS – PERSONAL PROPERTY

Limitations apply to the following personal property. These limits do not increase the amount of insurance under *Personal Property Coverage*:

Total Amount of Insurance in Any One Loss	Description of Personal Property Subject to Limitations
$250	Animals, birds, and fish
$250	Money, travelers checks, stored value cards, bank notes, bullion numismatic property, gold other than gold ware or gold-plated ware, silver other than silverware or silver-plated ware and platinum other than plantinumware
$1000	Theft of trading cards including sports cards
$2000	Accounts, bills, deeds, evidences of debt, letters of credit, notes other than bank notes, passports, securities, tickets, stamps and philatelic property
$2000	Trailers and campers not otherwise insured, whether licensed or not
$2000	Manuscripts
$2500	Property pertaining to a business actually conducted on the residence premises, including property in storage, held as samples, or held for sale or delivery after sale
$500	Business property away from the residence premises, regardless of whether the business is conducted on or away from the residence premises
$3000	Theft of guns and related equipment
$3000	Theft of jewelry, watches, furs, precious and semi-precious stones
$3000	Theft of silverware, silver-plated ware, goldware, gold-plated ware and pewterware
10% of Personal Property Coverage	Personal property usually situated at any residence owned or occupied by anyone we protect other than a residence premises. Personal property in a newly-acquired principal residence is not subject to this limitation for the 30 days immediately after you begin to move property there.

Figure 6:3 Extraction Sample – Categorical Limits

Some special limits on coverage may apply to only specific types of loss causes such as those losses resulting from theft, while others may apply to all losses.

Example: $3,000   Theft of jewelry, watches, furs, precious and Semi-precious stones

If the loss is a result of theft, the policy will only provide settlement for the first $3,000 of loss incurred from the theft of jewelry, watches, furs or precious and semi-precious stones regardless of the total value of the loss or the maximum personal property coverage limitations

If the loss is a result of another covered peril, such as a fire, the policy provides settlement for all items within this category up to the maximum personal property coverage limitations of the policy

The specific limitations will be detailed within the wording of the policy. It is important that you define any applicable limitations for the insured so that they have the correct expectations of the settlement of the claim.

INVENTORY

The insured must compile an inventory those personal items that are damaged because of the loss. The inventory will be a detailed analysis of all personal property and should include

- a description of the item

- the quantity of each item damaged

  Example: 4 chairs

- the age of the item

- the purchase value of the item

- the date of purchase

- the method of payment at the time of purchase

If personal property is insured on an actual cash value basis, the insured may be required to provide proof of the value of the items in question. The insured may need to provide

- photographs of the item

- purchase receipts

- owner's manuals

- other documentation that proves the items specifics and value

You will have access to a depreciation program that enables you to enter the basic data pertaining to each piece of personal property and obtain a current market value. If the insured provides adequate proof that the item listed on the inventory sheet existed, you may be able to reach an agreement with the insured regarding the ACV of the personal property based on the results of the depreciation program.

The insured should be provided with the applicable forms to assist in the inventory processes. You should request that any bills, receipts or other proof of value relating to each item claimed on the personal property form be copied and attached to the final inventory sheet. These proofs will assist in minimizing disputes pertaining to the value of each entry and in streamlining the settlement process.

1	2	3	4	5	6	7	8	9	10
QTY	Product Item Desc	Mfg	Model Number	Options / Features	Where Purchased	Date Purchased	Means of Purchase	Age	Value Claimed
1									
2									
3									
4									
5									

Figure 6:4 Sample Personal Property Inventory Form

The personal property inventory from will begin with a statement regarding concealment or fraud that serves as a reminder to the insured that any act on their part proven to be fraudulent, including the misrepresentation of personal property ownership, damage, value or condition may be punishable by law.

Columns one through six provides an area for the insured to detail the specifics of the personal property they are claiming under the loss.

1 QTY
    1
    2
    3

Column one provides a numbering system for the inclusions of the page and also enables the insured to consolidate the entries by listing multiple items that are the exact same in all details within one entry field.

Example: Qty 2 Description: Kitchenette Chairs

2
Product
Item
Description

Column two provides an area to enable the insured to provide both a general name and detailed description of each item claimed as damaged or destroyed as a result of the covered loss.

It is important that the insured understand that the description of the item needs to be as detailed as possible. These descriptive details assist in the proper valuation of each item entered on the form.

3
Manufacturer

Column three enables the insured to provide manufacturer information or other brand identifiers for the applicable item. This information will assist in evaluating the market value or replacement cost value of the item.

4
Model
Number

The insured should enter specific model numbers for any item to which these numbers would be applicable.

All electronic appliances and many other household items will include such identifying numbers.

If the damages to the item are extensive, the insured may find these numbers on owner's manuals, receipts, or packaging. The records of the store that sold the product to the insured may contain model information if the item is a warranty-based item or if the purchase was recent.

5
Options/Features

Specific options and features applicable to the item may effect the final value determination. The insured should enter as many details regarding enhancing options or product features as possible to assist with the valuation processes.

> Example: Digital, Picture-In-Picture System with Surround Sound

The more detailed the options and features segment of the loss inventory, the more concise the final valuation of that item will be during the depreciation and settlement portion of the claims process.

6
Where
Purchased

The insured may not know the purchase venue of many of the items entered on the loss summary. The purchase venue of more expensive items will often be easier to recall than that of smaller, less expensive goods that might be included on the personal property loss list.

This column often serves as a verifier column for the value of a specific entry. The need to complete this entry for larger, more expensive items also helps to act as a fraud deterrent.

7
Date
Purchased

The insurer should enter the approximate date of purchase or age each item. The date of purchase will verify the age field entered later in the form and make the ability to track down a questionable purchase easier if you have the need to conduct purchase research at some point in the future.

You will use the date of purchase and the approximate age entered by the insured as the baseline for depreciation calculations.

8
Means of
Purchase

The insurer should enter the method of payment that was used to make the purchase of the applicable item.

This information can be used to verify the existence of an item if a question arises relating to the claim.

This information may sometimes be used to obtain proof of the value or cost of an item at the time of purchase through data included on the credit receipt or within the books of the purchase establishment.

9
Age

The insurer should enter the approximate age of the applicable item. The age should correspond to the date of purchase for all items that were new at the time of purchase. The age may vary from the date of purchase if the applicable item was purchased in used condition or is considered an antique or collectible type of good.

The age of the item will act as the baseline for the depreciation of value calculations.

10
Value
Claimed

The insurer should enter the amount that they believe the item is worth.

It is important that you define the difference between actual market value and replacement cost value. You should define the settlement methods that you will apply in relationship to the claim.

If you will use actual cash value for settlement of the claim, the insured should gain an understanding of the methods and data that apply to the value determinations.

If you will use replacement cost value for settlement of the claim, the insured should gain an understanding of the requirements to obtain the replacement cost of an item claimed under the loss.

FOR COMPANY USE ONLY

Replacement Cost	Actual Cash Value	Repairs Only

The insurer or adjuster will enter the value of each entry on the personal property inventory sheet. These values will be based upon

- settlement method
- depreciation calculations applied
- replacement cost discounts that the insurer may obtain when replacing an item
- the expected costs to repair an item claimed

Each field should be complete. This helps to ensure that the insured has an understanding of the basis of the final determination for settlement. The completion of all option value calculations helps to minimize the potential settlement costs to the insurer by ensuring that the most cost effective option is illustrated.

CHAPTER

7

Insured Actions

Each policy contains conditions that the insured must follow to prevent claims, mitigate losses resulting from a claim and to facilitate the claims processes.

The policy will state the actions that the insured must take following a loss to fulfill their duties with regard to the loss. The actions of the insured after a loss are essential for protecting the interests of all parties in the claim. Prompt action on the part of the insured helps to minimize future disputes regarding the claim by minimizing additional damages suffered post-claim that may not qualify for coverage under the terms of the policy.

WHAT TO DO WHEN A LOSS HAPPENS

In case of a loss, anyone we protect must:

give us or our Agent immediate notice of the loss . If the loss is due to criminal activity or theft, you must notify the police;

do whatever possible to recover and protect the property from further damage. If it is necessary to protect the property, you must make reasonable repairs and keep a record of all repair costs,

furnish a complete inventory of damaged property including quantity, actual cash value and amount of loss claimed,

produce for examination, with permission to copy, all books of accounts, bills, invoices, receipts, other vouchers and other financial information as we may reasonably require;

show us or our representative the damaged property, as often as may be reasonably required;

at our request, separately submit to examinations and statements under oath and sign a transcript of same;

cooperate with us in our investigation of a loss and any suits;

send to us, within 60 days after our request, your signed and sworn proof of loss statement.

Figure 1:3   Extraction Sample – Insured Duties

NOTICE

The insured must notify the insurer of a loss promptly after the loss occurs. This notice may be a verbal contact with the insured's agent or claims office. If the policy specifically stipulates a requirement for written notice, it is essential that you counsel the insured to provide this notice to the insurer as soon as possible.

The insured must also notify the police, fire, or other service personnel when applicable.

- If a loss is a result of a theft, the insured should contact the local police office and file a report that will enable the police to begin investigating the theft.

  This speedy notice ensures that the police have the ability to begin the investigation promptly have a higher likelihood of recovering the stolen property

  The requirement to file a report with a legal authority helps to deter fraudulent claims. The completion of a report also enables the insurance company to notify the applicable department of their interest in the stolen property and may present an opportunity for the insurer to recover settlement costs if the stolen property is recovered by the police later.

- If a loss is a result of a fire, the insured should obtain the assistance of the fire department as soon as possible to assist in limiting the extent of the damages.

  A speedy response by the fire department can contain the resulting damage to only one portion of a property. This prompt response helps to limit the costs to the insurer.

  The fire department will typically create a cause of fire report that could be useful to the insurance adjuster in determining the cause of the fire, isolating fraud indicators, and determining whether the cause was a peril covered under the policy.

PROTECTION

The insured has a reasonability to take reasonable action to protect the property against further damage or loss.

Example: If the claim is a result of a fire, the insured may need to board up the entry or venting points used by the fire personnel when they were fighting the fire at the property.

Often windows or doors will be broken when firefighters are attempting to halt the spread of a fire or vent the smoke resulting from the fire.

The homeowner must take reasonable steps to ensure that the property is secured against theft, weather related damage or other post-cause damages.

Example: If the claim is the result of a water matter, the insured may need to shut off the water supply to the property, remove wet or damaged personal property and install fans to begin the drying process and halt the growth of mold and mildew until such time as the clean up and restoration work can commence.

The insured should keep a record of all repairs that have been made relating to providing protection of the property. These reasonable and necessary repairs will typically become a part of the loss settlement. The records of the insured should include the repair or protection act conducted the reason for the action, and the receipts for any applicable materials or services relating to this repair or protection activity.

INVENTORY

The insured must compile an inventory those personal items that are damaged because of the loss. The inventory will be a detailed analysis of all personal property damaged as a result of the peril.

The completion of the personal property inventory forms is defined in the chapter relating to the personal property element of the course.

ACCESS

The insured must provide you or another representative of the insurance company with access to the damaged property as often as is deemed necessary to complete the claims process. This access enables the insurer to verify the cause and amount of the loss. This access also enables the insurer to verify the status of any repair or restoration work being completed or to verify additional loss discoveries made during the repair or restoration process.

PROOF OF LOSS

The insured must provide a signed and witnessed or notarized proof of loss document. This document details the information about the cause of the loss, the costs of the loss and the satisfaction of the parties involved in the loss.

PROOF OF LOSS

Concealment or Fraud
We do not provide coverage for any insured who has intentional concealed
Or misrepresented any material fact or circumstance to this insurance.

CLAIM NUMBER

1.   Under policy #_____ , issued to (insured) _____
_____ (I or we) _____ hereby make claim for ($_____)
_____ Dollars.

2.   On or about the _____ day of _____ , 20_____ , at or about the hour of
_____ AM/PM, a loss occurred under the following circumstances.

STATE HOW, WHEN AND WHERE LOSS OR DAMAGE OCCURRED
(FULL DETAILS REQURED)

_____
_____
_____

The property described belonged at the time of loss to _____
_____
and no other person or persons had any interest therein; except: _____
_____

Was there other insurance on the property for which claim is being made hereunder __ Yes __ No Describe Property
_____ Amount of other
insurance $_____ other company _____

If claim is for theft, pilferage or larceny, state whether the police or authorities were advised __ Yes __ No
When_____ Where_____

Any other information that may be required will be furnished on call, and considered part hereof.

The said loss did not originate by any act, design, or procurement on the part of anyone we protect. Any other information that may be required will be furnished and considered part of this proof.

In consideration of any payment made from this proof, the undersigned hereby assigns and transfers to
_____ and agrees that _____ is subrogated to each and all claims and demands against any person, firms, or corporations arising from or connected with such loss or damage to

the extent of the amount of such payment. The undersigned agrees he will assist _____ in the prosecution of such claims and will execute any and all papers necessary in effecting recovery.

It is expressly understood and agreed, that the furnishing of this blank to the Insured or the preparing of proofs by the adjuster, or any Agent of _____ is an act of courtesy and not a waiver of any rights of _____.

NOTICE: Any person who knowingly and with intent to defraud any insurance company or other person files an application for insurance or statement of claim containing any materially false information or conceals for the purpose of misleading information concerning any fact material thereto commits a fraudulent insurance act, which is a crime and subjects the person to criminal and civil penalties.

Figure 7:1 Sample – Proof of Loss

Concealment or Fraud
We do not provide coverage for any insured who has intentional concealed
Or misrepresented any material fact or circumstance to this insurance.

Figure 7:2 Sample – Proof of Loss Extraction

The proof of loss form will typically contain a concealment or fraud warning notice to the insured. The proof of loss is a legal document signed by the insured attesting to the cause, extent, and satisfaction relating to the loss claim. It is critical that any instances of concealment or fraud on the part of the insured or an individual receiving financial benefit in the claims process be thoroughly investigated. By incorporating this clause into the final proof of loss form, the insurer retains the right to use this document if facts are discovered in the future that indicate that the insured committed an act of concealment or fraud relating to the claim.

1.   Under policy #_____, issued to (insured) _____
_____ (I or we) _____ hereby make claim for ($_____)
_____ Dollars.

Figure 7:3 Sample – Proof of Loss Extraction

The specifics of the policy and insured individual's legal names will be entered onto the form.

2.   On or about the _____ day of _____, 20_____, at or about the hour of
_____ AM/PM, a loss occurred under the following circumstances.

STATE HOW, WHEN AND WHERE LOSS OR DAMAGE OCCURRED
(FULL DETAILS REQUIRED)

_____
_____
_____

Figure 7:4 Sample – Proof of Loss Extraction

The insured will enter the specific date, time that the loss occurred, and then detail the cause of loss in their own words. The details of the cause of loss should be compared to any other statements of cause provided by the insured to ensure that all of the entries and statements are comparable. If any discrepancies in the statements of cause exist, additional inquiry may be needed to ensure that the cause of loss is covered under the policy and that no instances of concealment or fraud have occurred in relationship to the claim. When the insured completes the proof of loss form, they are swearing that the facts set forth on the form are true to the best of their knowledge. If the insured remit a proof of loss and it is proven that, the entries are untrue, the insured will have committed an act of material misrepresentation, and the insurer may have cause to deny the claim.

The property described belonged at the time of loss to _____
_____
and no other person or persons had any interest therein; except: _____
_____

Figure 7:5 Sample – Proof of Loss Extraction

The insured will be asked to confirm the interested parties to the claim and attest that no other parties exist who may have held interest in the damaged item(s). This protects the insurer against future claims by an undisclosed interested party.

Was there other insurance on the property for which claim is being made hereunder __ Yes __ No

---

Figure 7:6 Sample – Proof of Loss Extraction

The insured will be asked to confirm that no other insurance exists in relationship to the claim. If other coverage exists that provides for loss payment, the settlement will need to be reconsidered based upon the coverage parameters of each policy and the applicability of any additional insurance held by the insured. During the initial interview, any secondary or additional coverage that exists in relationship to the claim should have been discovered. This question on the proof of loss form confirms the information obtained at the initial interview and allows for a legal confirmation regarding any other insurance coverage.

The said loss did not originate by any act, design, or procurement on the part of anyone we protect. Any other information that may be required will be furnished and considered part of this proof.

A final statement of cause will be incorporated into the proof of loss form. This statement provides a legally witnessed and binding confirmation that the insured did not cause the loss in some manner and acts as a supporting document in the event that an act of fraud or concealment of cause is determined at some future point in time.

In consideration of any payment made from this proof, the undersigned hereby assigns and transfers to _____ and agrees that _____ is subrogated to each and all claims and demands against any person, firms, or corporations arising from or connected with such loss or damage to the extent of the amount of such payment. The undersigned agrees he will assist _____ in the prosecution of such claims and will execute any and all papers necessary in effecting recovery.

Figure 7:7 Sample – Proof of Loss Extraction

The insured will guarantee to provide any assistance and support necessary to the insurer if any other individual, corporation, or firm is found to be partially or fully liable for any part of the loss claim. This section transfers the rights of recovery against any party subject to prosecution or recovery by the insurer.

NOTICE: Any person who knowingly and with intent to defraud any insurance company or other person files an application for insurance or statement of claim containing any materially false information or conceals for the purpose of misleading information concerning any fact material thereto commits a fraudulent insurance act, which is a crime and subjects the person to criminal and civil penalties.

Figure 7:8 Sample – Proof of Loss Extraction

A final notice regarding fraud and concealment will often be incorporated into the proof of loss form to maximize the standing of the insurer if it is discovered in the future that the insured committed fraud or concealed information relating to the claim, cause of loss or other matter that effects the rights of the insurer.

The insured should provide the proof of loss early during the adjustment process. The inclusions of the proof of loss commit the insured their versions of the material facts of the claim. This form will be critical to any instance of fraud or concealment discovered during the investigation and adjustment of the claim.

You should verify the time requirement for the proof of loss with the company for whom you are completing adjusting function. Once the insured has remitted the final proof of loss to you, the claim settlement must be finalized within a specified period of time. Some insurers will choose to place the timing of the proof of loss requirement later in the claims process to minimize potential delays that may occur during adjustment and maximize the likelihood that the claim will be settled in compliance with fair and timely handling requirements. Other insurers will require the proof of loss to be remitted by the insured early in the adjustment process to maximize the position of the insurer if material facts or investigative information point to potential arson or fraud.

The settlement timing requirements after receipt of the proof of loss will typically be dictated by Statute. You should refer to the internal manual of the insurer and review the Statutes applicable within your state to determine the timeline that you must follow with regard to claim adjustment and settlement practices.

Upon receipt of the proof of loss, the insurer must take one of two actions:

1. Accept the proof of loss and proceed to claim settlement

2. Reject the proof of loss and request the insured modifies the unacceptable inclusions within the proof so that the insurer may issue a claim denial or settlement

If the proof of loss is rejected by the insurer, the rejection must be provided to the insured within statutorily defined timelines. The notice must define the specific reason for the rejection.

Example: the proof of loss does not contain sufficient insured
explanation regarding the cause of the loss

This rejection provides the opportunity for the insured to modify the inclusions of the proof of loss and remit it for a second review. A lack of sufficient descriptive cause verbiage will typically be considered an honest mistake on the part of the insured. Most courts will allow the insured to modify or amend a proof of loss where the changes will be the result of an honest mistake. If the rejection is based upon an honest mistake, the insured will have the opportunity to correct the proof of loss and resubmit it to the insurer. The acceptance of the modified proof of loss supersedes the inclusions of the original proof of loss. Acceptance of a modification on the part of the insured often negates the ability of the insured to deny the claim based on the original proof of loss inclusions.

EXAMINATION UNDER OATH

Not all claims will require that the insured undergo an examination under oath, however nearly every policy reserves the right to require that the insured do so if necessary.

The examination under oath is an invaluable tool when you are unable to obtain necessary claim settlement information from

- the insured

- witnesses

- legal reports

- other sources

- or when arson or fraud is suspected in a claim

The examination under oath is a process where the insured provides specific answers to questions presented regarding the claim, the cause, or the actions of the insured. The examination under oath provides the insurer with the extra information that may be needed to make a final determination as to whether they will cover or deny the claim.

If you feel that an examination under oath may be necessary to complete the processes of a claim, you should instigate the process as early as possible. If you are going to require that the insured submit to an examination under oath, you must ensure that they understand that this is a requirement of the claims process and not a request on the part of the insurer.

CONDITIONS OF EXAMINATION

It is important that you understand that you can require that the insured submit to an examination under oath as part of the policy coverage requirements. You also have the right to demand that any additional individual who is claiming rights of coverage under the policy submit to the examination depending on the wording of the policy.

Additional individuals not holding an interest in the claim settlement may be requested to submit but cannot be forced to do so.

Before demanding or requesting that any individual submit to the examination under oath, you should review the exact wording of the policy to ensure that you understand who can be required to submit and who has the right to decline the demand or request.

When you demand that an insured submit to an examination under oath, you must provide a specific date, time, and location for the examination. This date, time, and location must be reasonably accessible for the person undergoing the examination.

When you choose the date and time for the examination, you must ensure that the insured has adequate time to prepare for the examination.

EXAMINATION LEGAL REQUIREMENTS

The demand for an examination under oath must contain specific inclusions to be legally binding. The demand letter must

- clearly state the insurer's intent to conduct an examination under oath with the insurer or other party

- detail the exact date, time, and location of the examination

- include the name of the individual who will conduct the examination

- Detail the contact information of the individual the insured can contact regarding the examination must be included within the letter. This enables the insured to confirm the details of the date, time, and location of the examination or to notify the insurer if an event occurs that prohibits the insured from attending on the designated date and time.

- detail any documents or proof items that the insured must bring to the examination

---

Claim No.   : 010100
Policy No.   : Q58-12
Date of Loss : June 17, 2060

Dear _____ :

    Our law firm represents _____ with respect to a loss which occurred to your property on or about June 17, 2060. _____ is at this time requiring that you submit to an examination under oat pursuant to the terms and conditions of the insurance contract at which time we will inquire further into the facts and circumstances of your loss as well as any other information deemed to be relevant to a claim determination. For purposes of the statement under oath, we would ask that you bring with you any documentation that has been previously requested by _____ as well as any other documentation that you believe will assist _____ in adjusting this claim.

    As the examination under oath is a policy requirement, I look forward to hearing from you with respect to the scheduling of the same and please be advised that nothing in this letter is intended to waive or alter any of the terms, conditions or defenses under the policy of insurance in question, all of which are expressly reserved and reaffirmed.

Figure 7:9   Sample – Examination Request Letter

The demand letter should be reviewed to insure that it contains all of the necessary binding information. If the demand letter is improperly created, the demand for the examination may not be enforceable. It is important that you consult with your supervisor before undertaking an examination under oath in any claim process.

EXAMINATION PROCEDURES

Any insured that is requested to submit to an examination under oath must appear in person at the date, time, and location specified within the letter. They will be asked to provide oral testimony regarding the material facts of the claim. A court reporter will be present at the examination to record the statements of all parties who are present. The insured should be counseled that they have the right to have their attorney present during the examination.

A representative of the insurance company will put questions relating to the claim to the person being examined. If the individual being examined has an attorney present to represent their interest and rights, the attorney may object to any question based on whether the question is material to the claim.

Example: A material questions is one that provides information that relates directly to the claim.

- the cause and amount of the loss

- the insured's actions or whereabouts at the time of the loss

- information about any previous losses the insured has suffered

- any financial matters relating to the insured or other interested party making a claim under the loss

An attorney present at the examination to represent the interest of the individual being examined will not be able to any question that is material to the claim, may not provide evidence on behalf of the insured or other interested party, and may not cross-examine any party to the examination.

Each question that is deemed to be material to the loss must be answered by the individual being examined.

The examination should be completed during one session. If the examination cannot be completed during the single session set forth in the record, a continuance must be read into the official record being kept by the court reporter. The time, date, and location of the continuance must also be read into the record so that a record exists proving that all parties present are aware of the terms of the continuance.

When the examination is completed, the record kept by the court reporter will be printed in the form of an official transcript. The person who conducted the interview on behalf of the insurer will review the transcript and provide the document to the individual being examined for review. Upon completion of the review, the individual being examined will sign the transcript confirming the inclusions.

Once the official transcript has been signed by the individual under examination, the examination under oath is considered to be complete.

EXAMINATION EXCEPTIONS

At times, issues may occur within the standards of the examination under oath. The handling of the exception to the standard practice will depend on the policy of the insurer for whom you are completing adjusting functions, the Statutes applicable to the claim.

If the individual being examined does not appear at the designated date, time, and location set forth in the request letter the insurer has two options regarding the handling of the exception.

1. Determine Statutes pertaining to the failure of the examinee to appear for questioning. Some States do not allow the examinee the option of failing to appear. If the Statutes dictate that appearance is mandatory without exception, the claim may be denied.

    If the Statutes dictate that the claim may be denied based upon the failure of an individual subject of the examination to appear at the designated time, date, and place, a reservation of rights letter should be sent. This letter states that the claim is being denied because the insured has violated the terms of the policy contract.

2. Determine if the individual being examined filed a rescheduling request for cause. Some States allow the examination to be rescheduled by either party if the reason for the adjustment to the schedule is valid.

   If the individual subject to examination filed a rescheduling request, a letter stating that the individual must contact the insurer to reschedule the examination should be sent.

The handling of a failure to appear will depend on the protocol of the insurer and the applicable Statues. You should review the internal guidelines of the insurer to confirm that the proper response is applied to any exception to the examination under oath standards.

The demand letter may indicate that the individual being examined must bring certain documentation to the examination. If the individual does not bring the specified documentation to the examination, the insurer may

- proceed with the examination without the documentation

- complete the portion of the examination possible without the applicable documentation and then reschedule the examination through the processes of continuance so that the requested documentation may become part of the official record

- halt the examination immediately by stating for the record that the individual subject to the examination under oath did not bring the requested documentation and then reschedule the examination for another date and time

When an exception occurs relating to an examination that is part of your claims process, you should contact the claims management supervisor to ensure that all of the necessary steps are completed according to the regulations and practices of the insurer for whom you work. The determination of the steps that will be taken with regard to the exception should be made by a senior claims examiner or a representative from the administrative offices of the insurer. You should not make the determination of the correct handling of an unusual examination situation without the input of these individuals.

CHAPTER

8

Claims Management and Closure

You will manage all of the elements of the claims process to ensure that the claim is settled in a reasonable time and in a manner that is fair to all of the involved parties.

The tasks necessary to reach claim settlement are varied and detailed. An essential element to the success of a property claims adjuster is the ability to master all of the tasks necessary to achieve the fair and timely claim settlement.

You will manage the claim process including

- reviewing all loss report details

- correlating coverage to the specifics of the claim

- investigating claim cause

- isolating potential fraud indicators

- ensuring insured understanding of the claim adjusting and settlement processes

- providing advance payments

- ensuring temporary housing is available for the insured

- meeting timelines on restoration work

- overseeing financial disbursements

Each element of the adjusting activity enables the claims process to flow to a smooth conclusion. Upon completion of the claims process, you will obtain signatures from the insured that enables you to close the file and move onto the next claim assigned to your roster.

Each element of the claims process has the potential to create additional work requirements that you will need to address. The sample claims process overview details the claims process best-case scenario. It is important that you gain the ability to address any matter that arises with regard to each claim assigned to you for completion.

APPLICATION OF DEDUCTIBLE

The deductible that will apply to the claim will be listed within the policy binder information. The deductible requires that the insured offset a specific portion of the loss through a payment on their own behalf.

This requirement helps to maximize the potential that the policyholder will act in a manner that minimizes claims because any claim will result in a cash outlay or loss in the amount of the deductible. The deductible also minimizes the number of claims the insurer will be required to handle. Many small claims will amount to less than the amount of the deductible and many insurers will hesitate to file a claim unless their loss will be offset by the insurer.

We will pay for loss minus the deductible shown on the **Declarations**. Unless otherwise provided in an endorsement, in the event of total loss to the *Dwelling* from a covered peril, the deductible will not apply.

The deductible does not apply to:

1.   *Loss of Use Coverage*

2.   *Credit Card, Charge Plate, Check Forgery and Counterfeit Money Protection*

3.   *Fire Department Service Charges*

4.   Fire Extinguisher Recharge

5.   *Lock Replacement After Loss*

Figure 8:1   Extraction Sample - Deductible Application

The deductible is typically not collected from the insured as a cash payment. The deductible will typically be subtracted from any loss settlement figure before the payment is made by the insurer.

Example:	Personal Property Loss Total	$2785
	Policy Deductible	$ 250
	Personal Property Loss Settlement	$2535

At times, the claim amount will reach the maximum limitations of the policy. When this happens, some insurers will apply the deductible to the total loss amount before applying the maximum coverage limitations. In other words, if the claim amount exceeds the maximum policy coverage by at least the amount of the deductible, the insurer will credit the deductible figure before applying the maximum loss limitations and thus absorb the amount of the deductible.

Example: **Straight Calculation**

Personal Property Loss Limit $32,500

Personal Property Loss Claim	$32,800
Settlement Amount	$32,500
Deductible Due	$ 250
Actual Settlement Check	$32,250
Loss to insured	$ 550

Deductible Offset Calculation

Personal Property Loss Limit	$32,500
Personal Property Loss Claim	$32,800
Policy Deductible	$ 250
Personal Property Loss Claim	$32,550
Settlement Amount	$32,500
Loss to Insured	$ 50

SETTLEMENT

One of the final steps to all claims processes is the remittal of the settlement payment. Settlement payments will often be segmented by the type of coverage applicable to the payment being made.

When a claim involves the dwelling and the mortgagee clause applies, any settlement checks remitted will typically require the signature of both the insured and the mortgagee of the property.

The mortgagee may disperse the claims settlement funding based upon periodic inspections and work scope milestones. The full claim settlement amount may be provided to the mortgagee and then the mortgagee will disperse the periodic payments to the insured to enable them to make payment to the retained work service companies. These periodic payments will typically be made based on inspections conducted by a third party retained by the mortgagee to confirm that the work indicated on the scope you created is being completed in a timely and professional manner.

Upon completion of all of the work indicated on the scope, the insured and the restoration company may be required to remit additional paperwork to the mortgagee to ensure that the security interest of the mortgagee in the effected dwelling is protected.

WAIVER OF LIEN

STATE OF _____

COUNTY OF _____

For and in consideration of the sum of $_____, receipt of which is hereby acknowledged, the undersigned hereby waives and releases any and all liens, claims, or rights of liens upon the following described premises situated in _____ County, State of _____.

LOCATED AT:

Which the undersigned may have under the statutes of the State of _____ relating to mechanics liens or for any other reason whatsoever on account of labor or materials or both furnished by the undersigned upon said premises above-described or any building or construction thereon.

Dated this _____ day of _____, 20_____.

_____
(Contractor)

Figure 8:2 Sample – Waiver of Lien

CERTIFICATION OF THE COMPLETION OF REPAIRS

Total amount of claim: $_____

I/We hereby certify that all necessary repairs in connection with the damage sustained to property located at
_____ resulting from
(type of damage) _____, on (date of loss) _____ have been completed in a workman-like manner and that no Material or Labor Liens have been or will be incurred as a result of the labor performed or material used.

Subject property has now been restored to the condition existing prior to the date of damage.

Dated this _____ day of _____, 20_____.

_____
(Mortgagor)

Subscribed and sworn before me this _____ day of _____ 20_____.

_____
(Notary Public)

My commission expires: _____

Figure 8:3 Sample – Certification of Repairs

LOSS DISCREPANCY

If you are unable to reach an agreement with the insured regarding the extent or costs of the loss, many policies enable either party to request that an appraisal be completed by a third party to settle the dispute.

The appraisal clause deals only with the amount or extent of the claim and does not address issues relating to the coverage of the policy or the interpretation of specific policy inclusions or exclusions.

APPRAISAL

If you and we fail to agree on the amount of loss, on the written demand of either, each party will choose a competent appraiser and notify the other of the appraiser's identity within 20 days after the demand is received. The appraisers will select a competent and impartial umpire. If the appraisers are unable to agree upon an umpire within 15 days after both appraisers have been identified you or we can ask a judge of a court of record in the state where your residence premises is located to select an umpire.

The appraisers shall then set the amount of loss. If the appraisers submit a written report of an agreement to us, the amount agreed upon shall be the amount of loss. If they cannot agree, they will submit their differences to the umpire. A written award by two will determine the amount of loss.

Each party will pay the appraiser it chooses, and equally bear expense for the umpire and all other expenses of the appraisal. However, if the written demand for appraisal is made by us, we will pay for the reasonable cost of your appraiser and your share of the cost of the umpire.

We will not be held to have waived any rights by any act relating to the appraisal

---

Figure 8:4 Extraction Sample - Appraisal

The appraisal clause dictates that either party may demand the services of an appraiser to resolve issues regarding valuation matters relating to the claim.

> The term a demand means that either party may force the use of an appraiser to resolve a difference of opinion and that the other party must comply with the demand and cannot refuse.

Provisions will be incorporated into the policy that defines the minimum qualifications required of any appraiser retained in relationship to the claim. Each party may choose to retain their own appraiser or one appraiser may be chosen to make a value determination.

Each appraiser retained in relationship to the issue will set a valuation or estimate of the costs of the matter in question. The appraiser will

- go to the loss site or receive the damaged item

- assess the item in question or overall damage of the claim

- calculate the amount of the loss based on this assessment

The assessments of each appraisal may vary in final value determination. These differences are due to variations in the repair or restoration approaches commonly used by the applicable appraiser. These cost variations can be likened to the bids provided by two different contractors for the same job. Each contractor will have preferred materials that they use for calculations and so their bids will vary some in the final costs.

These competitive appraisals provide a high and low estimate for the questionable loss item. The estimates can be factored to determine the final cost of the claim. Each estimate should contain items of similarity such as

- scope of work

- repair determination

- replacement determination

- the exact dimensions of the damaged area

- details of the damaged item

If two appraisers are retained and the final amounts dictated by the appraisals vary greatly in cost analysis, the policy appraisal provision will dictate the method of handling the matter. Most policy provisions state that both appraisals will be remanded to an umpire or mediator. This individual will issue a decision as to the validity of the appraisal figures and make a final determination as to the amount of the claim.

Once an appraisal process has been instigated, it is binding on both the insured and the insurer regardless of whose valuation determination ends up being upheld by the results of the appraisal. If one party believes that the appraisal presents a fraudulent assessment or a mistake, they may challenge the validity of the appraisal. Other circumstances for challenge may exist, but a senior claims manager will need to assess the situation to determine the validity of any more elaborate issues that arise.

The appraisal provision of the policy will dictate who will bear the costs of the appraisal. Costs can be borne by the individual demanding the completion of the appraisal, by each party independently retaining the services of the appraisal or in another manner. It is important that you review the policy wording to determine the assessment of appraisal costs.

FRAUD, MISREPRESENTATION, CONCEALMENT

If you suspect that the insurer is engaged in a criminal act such as arson or fraud, the claims processes will be interrupted while a determination is made as to the obligations of the insurer to the insured.

> Most policy wording states that if the insured is found to have engaged in fraud, misrepresentation of a claim, or concealment of material facts of the claim, the insurer is not obligated to make payment on the claim.

> Most policy wording also states that the insurer must not have taken action or caused action to be taken that created the claim. You will often suspect that an issue exists before you can prove that the insurer has perpetrated a crime or is participating in a fraudulent act.

If an act of fraud, misrepresentation, arson, or concealment has occurred, the insured may not be required to make payment for the resulting loss.

CONCEALMENT, FRAUD OR MISREPRESENTATION

This entire policy is void as to you and anyone we protect if, whether before or after a loss:

1.   you or anyone we protect have intentionally concealed or misrepresented any material fact or circumstance concerning this insurance; or

2.   there has been fraud or false swearing by you or anyone we protect as to any matter that relates to this insurance or subject thereof; or

3.   you or anyone we protect engage in fraudulent conduct as to any matter that relates to this insurance or subject thereof..

In the event of 1., 2., or 3. above, we will not pay for any loss.

Figure 8:5   Extraction Sample – Fraud, Misrepresentation, Concealment

Acts of fraud, concealment, or misrepresentation are three elements that you must always look for when opening and adjusting a claim.

- Fraud is the intentional act of deceit resulting from the false representation of the facts of a matter.

  Fraud occurs most often when an insurer exaggerates the loss sustained during a claim or when an insured intentionally causes the peril that created the claim.

- Arson is the most commonly encountered fraudulent act.

  Arson fraud occurs when the insurer causes the fire or has another individual cause the fire on their behalf but claims the occurrence is an accident.

  Arson may be suspected by the fire team called to the site of the claim, by you or brought forth by witnesses to the claim.

- Concealment is the intentional act of withholding pertinent details or information that the individual has a reasonable duty to disclose.

Acts of concealment commonly occur at the time of the initial insurance application.

The original application for coverage by the insured should be compared to the current statements of the insured to confirm that all matters agree.

An applicant may conceal pertinent details at the time that they apply for coverage to ensure that their application is accepted or in an attempt to lower the costs that will be assessed for the coverage.

Common occurrences of application concealment would be the statement that the insured has no pets when they in fact own a canine that is considered uninsurable or whose ownership often results in an increase in premium.

- Misrepresentation is the intentional statement of some matter as fact or true and correct when it is not a fact, truth or complete information.

An insured may intentionally or unintentionally make a statement that can be considered a misrepresentation of fact.

It is important that you gain the ability to sort through insured statements and learn when a statement warrants additional questioning and when it should be referred to a senior staff member for review and a determination of the best action.

Common misrepresentations include statements made by the insured regarding the value of a loss, claim, or insurance coverage history and the concealment of another insurance policy that provides coverage to the insured.

Fraud is one of the most serious coverage defenses that you and the insurer can bring against an insured. This is a serious allegation that essentially states the insurer's belief that the insured has committed a crime.

If you have reason to suspect fraud, concealment, misrepresentation, or intentional damage on the part of the insurer, you should consult with a senior claims examiner. They will provide you with the assistance necessary to determine the steps the insurer wishes to take with regard to the claim. Fraud investigations will often require the hiring of a specialized investigator, include a demand for an examination under oath, and may include other remedies common to the practices of the insurer for whom you work.

If it is discovered and proven that the insured committed an act of fraud, concealment, or misrepresentation, the policy wording will dictate the handling of the claim. In most cases, the insurer will not be obligated to make any payment on a claim where it is proven that the insured committed one of these acts.

Before the policy coverage can be denied based on fraud, concealment, or misrepresentation, the act must be proven to have occurred. The act must also be proven to have been intentional.

If you suspect that an insured is engaging in an act that may void the policy coverage, you should consult with a senior adjuster to determine the steps and actions that will be taken to prove the case against the insured.

It is actually the duty of the insured to provide proof that the claim is a result of a peril covered under the policy components.

> As the adjuster, you will often fulfill this obligation on behalf of the insured as part of your regular claims processing, but the burden rests on the shoulders of the insured making the claim.

> If the loss were a result of a fire, the insured would be required to prove that a fire occurred to fulfill their obligations under the policy.

It is the obligation of the insurer to prove that a specified claim or claim element is not covered because of specific policy exclusions.

> If the loss were the result of a fire whose cause was arson, the insured would prove the loss of a covered peril, namely fire.

> You would need to prove that the loss is excluded from coverage because the fire was a result of an act of attempted fraud.

To succeed in excluding or denying coverage due to arson, the insurer must prove that the fire was deliberately set and that the insured instigated the actions that caused the fire.

ARSON OR FRAUD INVESTIGATIONS

Any investigation into suspected arson or a fraudulent act on the part of the insured should be implemented as soon as you note any discrepancy that brings the concept of fraud into the claim.

Adjusters typically begin to suspect potential insurance fraud due to the manner or actions of the insured or because of physical evidence at the loss scene indicates the event did not occur in the typical manner.

If you suspect that a claim you are adjusting is a result of a fraudulent act, including potential arson, you must ensure that you obtain a non-waiver agreement from the insured or issue a reservation of rights letter to the insured to protect the interest of the insurer during the investigative phase.

A fraud indicator is described as a hint that a more detailed investigation should be made into the cause or activity surrounding an insurance claim. Fraud will typically take one of two forms.

- Fraud may be an act on the part of the insured or individual acting for the insured that has the appearance of being a part of the normal operations or activity at the claim location.

  These actions are often difficult to prove for the insurer as they give the appearance that the act that caused the claim was an inadvertent side effect of normal operations.

- Fraud may be an act that the perpetrator takes great care to conceal.

  This type of fraudulent activity typically dictates that the insured or individual acting on behalf of the insured intentionally creates the situation that caused the loss but made an attempt to conceal their actions.

These types of activities are often easier to isolate, as the action that caused the loss will be different from the normal activity at the loss location making it easier to spot.

You should familiarize yourself with common indicators of property fraud to ensure that you have the ability to isolate potential fraud and take proactive steps to protect the insurer and the insured.

Example: Insured has a higher than average knowledge of insurance claims process

Insured is willing to accept a smaller than normal settlement in return for a speedy closure of the claim

You should then work with your claims team to conduct two investigations into the claim. The first investigation will work toward proving that the loss resulted from a fraudulent act on the part of the insured. The second investigation will proceed in the same manner as all claims adjusting processes to ensure that if arson or fraud is not an element in the claim, all of the required activities necessary to resolve the claim quickly and efficiently are in place.

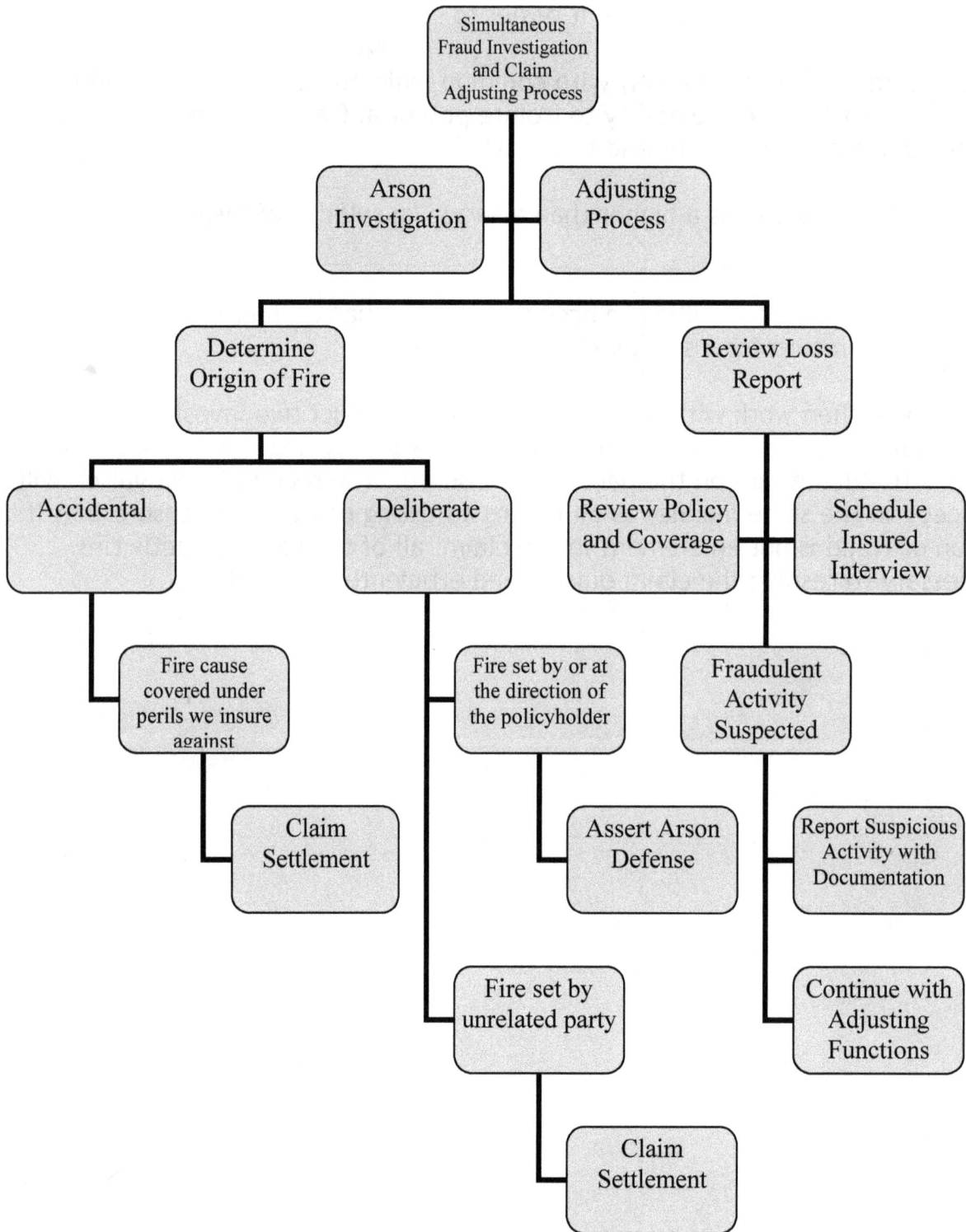

Simultaneous Fraud Investigation and Claim Adjusting Process

Arson Investigation

Adjusting Process

Determine Origin of Fire

Review Loss Report

Accidental

Deliberate

Review Policy and Coverage

Schedule Insured Interview

Fire cause covered under perils we insure against

Fire set by or at the direction of the policyholder

Fraudulent Activity Suspected

Claim Settlement

Assert Arson Defense

Report Suspicious Activity with Documentation

Fire set by unrelated party

Continue with Adjusting Functions

Claim Settlement

While the material facts of a claim relating to a suspected act of fraud, misrepresentation, or concealment are being gathered, you must act in a manner that ensures that you and the insurer are not acting in bad faith. You must also protect against inadvertently waiving the rights of the insurer to deny the claim.

> Bad faith is any act on the part of the insurer or representative of the insurer that misleads the insured, lengthens the claims process unjustly, or results in damages to the insured.
>
> A waiver is the relinquishments of a right through a voluntary or involuntary action or inaction.
>
> Example: If you have reason to believe the claim will be denied based on fraud, misrepresentation or concealment but state that the claim will be paid in discussion with the insured, you may be inadvertently denying the right of the insurer to deny the claim.

It is essential that you consult with a senior adjuster from the insurer before discussing the claim with the insured after you begin to suspect an issue exists. Additional details pertaining to the waiver of rights is incorporated into the adjuster advancement materials.

You can avoid acts of waiver, bad faith, or estoppels by taking steps to protect yourself during the claims process. You may

- instigate a reservation of rights letter

- have the insured sign a non-waiver agreement

- promptly process all claims assigned to you for adjusting

You will typically obtain a non-waiver agreement from the insured at the time of the initial meeting and many advance payment receipt forms contain non-waiver language.

RESERVATION OF RIGHTS

A reservation of rights letter is often used in the same manner as a non-waiver agreement but is presented to the insured in the form of a letter. The reservation of rights letter will contain the same general information, provisions, and details as the non-waiver agreement and serves to protect the insurers rights by detailing the specific policy provision or question that has arisen in the claims process.

The letter will detail the specific coverage part in question, the reason for the insurer's questions, and a statement that the insurer reserves the right to raise other coverage issues at a later time that are not detailed within the reservation of rights letter.

Many adjusters will attach the specific excerpt from the policy that applies to the matter in question to the reservation of rights letter. The reservation of rights letter may be delivered by hand or by certified mail. The insurer must be able to provide proof of the delivery of the letter.

These letters are typically used when you are not able to meet with all of the named insured of the policy in person or when a named insured has refused to sign a non-waiver agreement.

Non-Waiver of Rights

The failure to enforce at any time the provisions of the policy or to require at any time any performance by the other party of any of the provisions hereof shall in no way be construed to be a waiver of such provisions or to affect either the validity of these rights or any part hereof, or the right of either party to enforce each and every provision in accordance with its terms.

Figure 8:7   Sample Non-Waiver Verbiage

Once the policyholder has signed a non-waiver agreement or received a reservation of rights letter, the insurer or adjuster can begin the process of investigating the cause and extent of the loss without inadvertently waiving the rights of the insurer under the policy.

The results of the investigation conducted by the claims adjuster, claims examiner, or other individuals will be compiled into a report and provided to the senior claims adjuster or claims department of the insurer. The senior claims manager will then use the details of these investigations to make a determination as to the validity, amount, and coverage of the loss.

BAD FAITH

It is important that you remember that while the reservation of rights and non-waiver agreements provide you with the an enhanced investigative opportunity and claim settlement time, you must still process the claim within a reasonable and fair time period or you risk entering the realm of a bad faith issue.

> Bad faith is defined by specific rules, regulations, and laws that limit the acts that an insurer, adjuster, examiner, or other claims personnel may take with regard to the handling of a claim.

The claims adjuster is expected to act in good faith in the handling of all claims.

The details of the good faith actions on the part of the adjuster will be outlined within the

- policy wording

- law governing the claim

- unfair claims practices act

Any action on the part of the claims adjuster, examiner, or other insurer retainer that is deemed to be in bad faith may enable the insured to bring a legal suit against the insurer.

If a bad faith suit is brought against the insurer, the damages that the insured seeks will be beyond those of the claim or above those that could be obtained in a simple breach of contract suit. If the court finds that the insurer or its retainers committed an act of bad faith, it may award punitive damages to the insured.

CONTRACTUAL OBLIGATIONS

Each insurance policy outlines the specific obligations of each party.

> The duties of the policyholder and the insured are specifically outlined within the policy contract.

It is your obligation as the assigned adjuster to fulfill the duties of the insurer. You must

- investigate the claim in a timely and comprehensive manner

- assess fair value to all property damaged because of the claim

- pay the costs relating to the claim within a reasonable period as specified by the policy inclusions

If you fail to fulfill the contractual obligations of the policy, you and thus the insurer, may be deemed to be in breach of contract. The contract in this instance is the policy covering the loss.

If the insured brings a breach of contract suit against the insurer, the costs assessed on the claim will be in excess of the actual loss valuation but will typically be less than the costs assessed in a bad faith suit.

The actual costs assessed to the insurer in the event that the court deems that a breach of contract has occurred will vary depending on the state but commonly include

- attorney fees

- court costs

- prejudgment interest on the total claim amount

other charges may be assessed depending on the statute under which the judgment is being issued. It is essential that you conduct all claims adjusting activities within the parameters of good faith and contractual obligations.

UNFAIR CLAIMS PRACTICES

Each state has enacted acts that outline what is considered to be an unfair claims practice. The statutes will vary depending on the location where you conduct your adjusting duties but all of the statutes are designed to address and prohibit certain acts that are unfair or deceptive. These statutes commonly address three primary claims practices.

TIME

Many statutes define a specified time limit within which an insurer must respond to insured communications, requests, make payment on claims, or issue claims denials.

Any delay that exceeds what is defined as a reasonable time for response or action by the state in which you conduct your claims adjusting function may be considered an unfair claims practice. Common delays that fall within the unfair practices act include

- a delay in responding to the notice of a claim

- a delay in responding to communications or requests by the insured

- a delay in settling claims by requesting enhanced documentation or loss proof when the claim value is considered to be reasonably clear

- A delay in issuing payment when the insured has a reasonable expectation of receipt of the payment

COMMUNICATION

You must communicate with the insured from the moment you place the initial telephone call to schedule the insured interview. Communication for the insurance adjuster means to convey information to the insured and respond to the questions and concerns of the insured with factual information. You must

- define the specific coverage of the policy for the insured

- you must define any coverage exclusions for the insured

- outline the responsibility of the insured

- provide an explanation of the allocation of any payments made to the insured

- define the applicable documentation required to receive payments under the claim

- define the reasons for any denial of any part of the claim and outline the segment of the policy that addresses this denial

- ensure that the insured has the opportunity to exercise all rights granted to them under the policy, law or statute

CLAIM DENIAL

You must ensure that any claim denial complies with the terms of the policy and that the insured has the reference materials necessary to understand the basis of a denial of all or any part of the claim. You must

- explain the premise behind any claim denial issued on a loss

- reference the specific area of the policy under which the denial is being made

- justify any claim denial in writing so that it is understandable to a lay person

- fully define the inclusions and ramifications of any claim settlement or compromise made in relationship to the claim

These instances are not the only actions or inactions that could fall within the realm of unfair claims practices, but are the most common that are encountered within the industry.

You should review the specific acts applicable to the state in which you will conduct your adjusting activity and ensure that you gain a comprehensive understanding of what is considered a fair and an unfair practice within your area.

If you or the insurer for whom you work is found to engage in unfair practices on frequent basis or with a frequency higher than that of other insurers within your region, it may be determined that these unfair acts are regular business practices for your company.

If it is determined that your company or you as an adjuster commonly engage in what is deemed to be an unfair manner the state may issue fines, penalties, and sanctions against you and the company or limit your ability to conduct business within that state.

The Department of Insurance that governs insurance practices within each state will typically make the determination regarding whether a practice is deemed to be an unfair act. In some jurisdictions, the insured may bring a lawsuit in a court of law to obtain a damage award if they believe that you have engaged in unfair acts with regard to their claims process.

You will often be required to consult with a senior claims examiner, claims management team, or insurer attorney before you are allowed to deny any claim brought by an insured.

These individuals will be schooled in the strict processes and requirements necessary to deny a claim under the policy guidelines and statutory regulations.

To instigate a claims denial review, you should

- gather all of the initial claims data

- obtain a signed non-waiver agreement or confirm the delivery of a reservation of rights letter

- consult with your senior adjuster to confirm the procedures you must undertake

- finalize the claims investigation process

- remit the file to the applicable department or claims manager for review

The claim file inclusions will be reviewed and a determination of status will be issued.

The claims manager may decide to make payment on the claim in which case you will complete the adjusting processes following the same procedure you follow with all other claims.

The claims manager may decide to deny the claim.

If the claim is to be denied, a written denial letter will be issued that states the specific reason for the denial and incorporates the policy provisions under which the denial is being made.

The claims manager may deem it appropriate to file a declaratory relief action within the applicable court.

A declaratory relief action requests that the court review the evidence you have gathered in conjunction with other investigators retained to investigate the elements of the loss and issue a declaration or judgment that the insurer is not obligated to pay the claim.

The act of remitting the claim to the court system for review and judgment protects the insurer in the event that the law regarding the denial is unclear or if the loss value is exceptionally high.

GENERATING REPORTS

The claims management guide of the insurer will dictate the form, contents, format and reporting submission requirements that you should follow with regard to each claim assignment.

The periodic and final reports of the claim will document all of the activity of the adjusting process, illustrate the findings of all investigative practices, and define the claim resolution details. The period and final reports that you remit may be subject to review by the insurer's attorney if a suit is filed or by the state insurance authorities. It is essential that the reports

- be free of error

- define the timeline of the adjusting process

- illustrate a timely settlement of the claim

- contain clear and concise verbiage

- maintain accuracy

- minimize inflammatory or opinionated remarks

- illustrate good faith processing of the claim

The first report you will create is the preliminary report. This report should be completed immediately following the meeting with the insured or within one week of the receipt of the claim assignment if the insured is unavailable for in interview.

The preliminary report will define

- the date of the loss

- the date that the adjuster received the claim assignment

- all initial activity completed on the assignment including

- an initial contact with the insured

- an initial interview with the insured

- receipt of the loss summary and policy

- any coverage elements or questions that are apparent

- the initial inspection of the loss location or matter and applicable findings

- recommendations or requests for senior claims adjuster assistance or input

The preliminary report may contain additional inclusions such as a preliminary scope or copies of reports from legal authorities. The insurer may provide you with a base form for completion. This form will contain all of the required information fields necessary for the preliminary report. The preliminary report will typically not be as detailed or elaborate as future reports as the time of remittal is early in the adjusting process. When a claim is clearly defined and smaller in scope, the preliminary report may become the final report.

Period status reports will be completed throughout the adjusting process of larger claims. These status reports provide updated information on the progress of the claim process. These reports will typically appear more as a timeline of events than as a reporting of claim elements. The purpose of status reports is to maintain a record of action on the claim and to ensure that all matters are being addressed by the adjuster in a timely manner.

Period status reports may also contain adjusting summary data. Summary data will contain more detail and serve to summarize each action and element of the adjusting process. These status reports enable the insurer to take prompt action if the claim process appears to be varying from the normal or expected path or to approve or disapprove a potential claim action before the process proceeds further.

The summary report will typically follow a paragraph format where details are provided under specific claim categorization headings. The insurer may have a specific format that they require for summary reports.

STATUS SUMMARY

Insured: _____   Date of Report _____

Loss Location _____   Adjuster: _____

Claim No.: _____   Adjuster No.: _____

---

1. Assignment: *Provide notice of the date of assignment, method of notification, and insured statements within the initial loss report*

---

2. Enclosures: *Detail all items attached to the summary such as photographs, investigative reports, authority reports, witness statements, or scope inclusions*

---

3. Requests: *Define any special requests by insurer such as additional advance payment funds, coverage questions, or special circumstances*

---

4. Claim Estimate: *The estimated value of the claim by coverage category should be entered so that the insurer has adequate expectations of the size and scope of the loss*

5. Coverage Application *Each element of coverage that will apply to the claim settlement should be defined with specific entries relating to deductible figures, other insurance, and categorization of losses to be claimed, applicable coverage limits, and potential limit exceptions*

6. Interested Parties *Details relating to all interested parties of the claim should be defined and applicable coverage detailed. The means of discovery of each interested party must be included*

7. Cause *The determination of the cause of loss and the means of arriving at this determination, including specific professional information, should be included with any applicable investigative reports attached to the summary.*

8. Insured Loss Statement *Details of the statement provided by the insured should be included to enable the comparison between the final determination and the statements of the insured. Any contradictory statements made by the insured should be defined and include a date and time stamp*

9. Witness Statement

Details of any statement provided by a witness to the peril or actions immediately before and after the loss should be included to enable the comparison between all statements relating to the loss. Any contradictory statements made by any party should be defined and include a date and time stamp.

10. Scope / Estimate

Details of any preliminary or final scope or estimate of damages should be incorporated into the report. These details should include area of damage, construction materials required for restoration, extent of damage, settlement recommendation, and a list of any contractor estimates that have been received on the claim

11. Settlement Negotiation

The status of any negotiation or agreement with regards to a coverage settlement should be defined. This status update includes any scope approval, the remittal of any personal property inventory forms, or other documents that will facilitate the final settlement of the claim

12. Settlement Recommendations

Any recommendation by the adjuster regarding the method of claim settlement should be incorporated to enable the insurer to review the applicable supporting data. These recommendations should include any calculations, bids, estimates, or related materials that the adjuster has completed

13. Completed Activity *A detail listing of all tasks completed on the claim should be incorporated to assist the insurer in determining the timeline of the claim and to serve as proof of activity in the event that a question arises regarding the timely handling of the claim matters*

14. Settlement Status *All remaining tasks necessary to reach settlement should be included within the summary. If the task list is elaborate, a timeline of expected completion should be attached to ensure that all parties are in agreement regarding the adjusting process tasks and status of timeliness*

15. Comments *Any comments that you have relating to the loss events, claim, settlement processes, status or other matters that are not included in another section of the summary should be entered. Any matters that relate to the claim should be defined for the insurer*

8:9 Report Inclusion Explanation

You will begin the processes of compiling the report by gathering all of the documentation relating to the claim. You must gather information detailing

- Insured and Interested Party Details

- Coverage and Exclusion Parameters

- Material facts of the loss

  Statements of the insured

  Reports provided by legal authorities

  Investigative findings and summary reports

- Proof of the cause or origin of the peril

- Documentation of co-insurance or other insurance applicable to the claim

- Emergency repairs data and receipts

- Scope of loss repairs

- Personal property inventory forms

- Personal property valuation worksheets

- Proof of Loss

- Any applicable notices, disclosures, and forms

- Settlement Determination

- Risk Advice or Notes

The elements contained within each of these items will be complied into the reports that you generate throughout the claim process. These reports are essential to supporting your actions, minimizing the risk to the insurer, and maintaining exceptional claim settlement practices.

You will create the closing report when you have completed all of the functions necessary to investigate the claim and either issued a final settlement or claim denial. You may also be required to issue a final report detailing all activity to date if your adjusting services are no longer necessary for the claims process.

Adjuster Skill Analysis

The duties of an insurance claim adjuster are varied and take a myriad of skill sets, strengths, and abilities. Each element of the adjusting process will require that you apply a different facet of your professional skills. It is essential that you understand the duties and skills of successful insurance claims adjusters and determine the application of each of these to your personal strengths.

General tasks will apply to each claim that you adjust. Some claims may require more attention to specific tasks. It is important that you foster skills and abilities that enable you to conduct each adjusting activity with the professionalism expected from individuals within your industry. Your personality plays an essential role in determining what specific characteristics will apply to you in personal, career and higher stress situations.

The following pages will assist you in better understanding the inherent characteristics that apply to your specific personality type and sub-type. We encourage you to capitalize on the strengths inherent in your personality and to understand the potential roadblocks specific characteristics may create in your pathway to career success.

There are no true personality weaknesses in the information you are about to review. There is, however, incredible opportunity for understanding yourself, gaining the ability to create the environment that will assist you on the path to success, and modifying your behavior to minimize potential roadblocks.

The profiles will also assist you in learning how best to handle the diversity you will encounter in individuals you work with on a daily basis. The career of an insurance claim adjuster requires you to work with a diverse group of individuals each day. It is essential that you perform all of the duties of your career in a professional and competent manner. Understanding the effect that the characteristics of the individuals you will work with have on your personality will assist you in mitigating any negative impact that these elements may have and in maximizing your ability to relate to each person with whom you work.

Each of us has heard people make reference to a Type A personality. We say someone is a Dynamic Person or an Innovative Individual. Some of you may have been in situations where you are categorized as illustrating the characteristics one type of personality or another.

Do you know what the personality classifications mean?

Have you learned the characteristics that often relate to these personality classifications?

Do you know which category characterizes your personality?

Do you understand the benefits that can be gained by altering your environment and outside influences to bring forth certain aspects of your personality in specific situations and minimizing other, less effective characteristics?

We are going to review the various terms for personality typing popularized through the years and the characteristics that define these terms.

This section will provide you with valuable insight into the motivations, strengths, and general characteristics of each main personality type that you may encounter during the day.

You should be able to determine the influence each personality type will have on your ability to succeed. You will also learn what personality designation characterizes your primary and secondary typing and the actions you can take to assist you in using the benefits of your personality to assist you on the path to career success.

An important point that you should understand is that there are no wrong or right personality types.

> Each type of personality carries with it various strengths as well as obstacles.

> Years of research have provided tools that you can use to turn any obstacle inherent to your personality type into a strength.

Another point to keep in mind is that no person can be characterized as totally one personality type or another. We each have a primary classification and secondary classifications. Some of us even have a different classification under stress than we do when we feel relaxed. Today we will review only the primary classifications.

Each of the primary classifications can also be considered secondary classifications. Once you have completed the worksheets and designated your primary classification you can easily designate your secondary classification by calculating the second highest figure on your answer sheet. If you carry the course one-step further by reviewing how your primary and secondary classifications interact with each other, you can gain additional insight into your actions, motivational triggers, and even stress-related obstacles. Additional, advanced training is available that will assist you in identifying, honing and minimizing various aspects of your personality.

The first step in the process is to complete the question sheet that you will find on the following pages. You will be the only person who reviews the results so please, be honest with yourself. You will learn valuable information that will assist you in obtaining your goals and become better skilled at analysis of others leading to greater interpersonal success.

- Review each question and the descriptive words supplied

- Consider your behavior and actions as they relate to the work environment

- Circle the one word out of each group that best describes your actions during work related activities

1. When I arrive for work I feel: Eager Bold Introspective Content	**2. I work best when I am given:** Defined Goals Recognition Authority Routine
4. I want my supervisor to provide: Direct Answers Sincere Appreciation Freedom of Expression Specific Recognition	**4. Sometimes I focus too much on:** Details Influencing Others Obtaining Results Cooperation
5. My career must provide: Challenge Accuracy Interaction Stability	**6. I approach each task with:** Consistency Problem Solving Critical Analysis Motivation
7. Co-workers describe me as: Inspiring Amiable Stable Competitive	**8. When faced with an unusual idea I feel:** Receptive Impulsive Detailed Adventurous
9. My greatest strength is: Persistence Expression Self-Reliance Competence	**10. My team sees me as:** Decisive Diplomatic Cooperative Group Oriented

11. As a team leader my style is:	12. To motivate others I employ:
Inspirational Patient Logical Results Oriented	Conscientiousness Persuasiveness Consideration Directness
13. When I think about work I feel:	14. I work best with:
Eager Independent Self-Reliant Loyal	Predictable Routines Clear Expectation Challenge Freedom
15. Under pressure I sometimes become:	16. My conversational style is:
Outspoken Precise Detailed Inspiring	Chatty Amiable Rational Direct
17. When receiving a compliment I feel:	18. I am pleased when others say I am:
Modest Uneasy Poised Non-Committal	Accomplished Charming Logical Loyal
19. I enjoy the role of:	20. When completing a difficult task I become:
Entertainer Leader Listener Diplomat	Concise Determined Persuasive Amiable

21. I focus on:		22. I react to the problems of others with:	
Accuracy	Results	Emotion	Sympathy
People	Consistency	Decisiveness	Sensitivity

23. I sometimes forget to:		24. At business functions I am:	
Pace Myself	Request Recognition	Amiable	Social
Use Time Management	Think Outside the Box	Reserved	Intense

25. I am inspired by:		26. I may be too concerned with:	
Popularity	Peace	Status	Control
Perfection	Power	Comfort	Ability

27. I perform best when I am:		28. Sometimes I think I am too:	
Order Setting	Analyzing	Serious	Sensitive
Socializing	Perceiving	Insensitive	Excitable

29. I enjoy being described as:		30. When waiting to begin a new task I feel:	
Self-Confident	Aggressive	Impatient	Anxious
Relaxed	Conscientious	Exuberant	Humble

The letter that corresponds to your testing answers most frequently will be considered your primary personality characteristic.

1. When I arrive for work I feel: Eager S Determined C Introspective M Content P	2. I work best when I am given: Defined Goals M Recognition S Authority C Routine P

3. I want my supervisor to provide:
 	
Direct Answers C   Sincere
                      Appreciation P
 	
Freedom of   Specific
Expression S   Recognition M
	4. Sometimes I focus too much on:
	
	Details M Influencing Others
	                  S
	
	Obtaining Results C Cooperation P

5. My career must provide: Challenge C Accuracy M Interaction S Stability P	6. I approach each task with: Consistency P Problem Solving C Critical Analysis M Motivation S
7. Co-workers describe me as: Inspiring S Amiable P Stable M Competitive C	8. When faced with an unusual idea I feel: Receptive P Impulsive S Detailed M Adventurous C
9. My greatest strength is: Persistence M Expression S Self-Reliance C Competence C	10. My team sees me as: Decisive C Diplomatic M Cooperative P Group Oriented S

11. As a team leader my style is:		12. To motivate others I employ:	
Inspirational S	Patient P	Conscientiousness M	Persuasiveness S
Logical M	Results Oriented C	Consideration P	Directness C

13. When I arrive at work I feel:		14. I work best with:	
Eager S	Independent M	Predictable Routines S	Clear Expectations C
Self-Reliant C	Loyal P	Challenge D	Freedom I

15. Under pressure I sometimes become:		16. My conversational style is:	
Outspoken C	Precise P	Chatty S	Amiable P
Detailed M	Inspiring S	Rational M	Direct C

17. When receiving a compliment I feel:		18. I am pleased when others say I am:	
		Accomplished C	Charming S
Modest P	Uneasy C		
		Logical M	Loyal P
Poised S	Non-Committal M		

19. I enjoy the role of:		20. When completing a difficult task I become:	
Entertainer S	Leader C	Concise M	Determined C
Listener P	Diplomat M	Persuasive S	Amiable P

21. I focus on: Accuracy P Results C People S Consistency M	22. I react to the problems of others with: Emotion S Sympathy P Decisiveness C Sensitivity M
23. I sometimes forget to: Pace Myself C Request Recognition P Use Time Management S Think outside the Box M	24. At business functions I am: Amiable M Social S Reserved P Intense C
25. I am inspired by: Popularity S Peace P Perfection M Power C	26. I may be too concerned with: Status S Control C Comfort P Ability M
27. I perform best when I am: Order Setting C Analyzing M Socializing S Perceiving P	28. Sometimes I think I am too: Serious M Sensitive P Insensitive C Excitable S
29. I enjoy being described as: Self-Confident S Aggressive C Relaxed P Conscientious M	30. When waiting to begin a new task I feel: Impatient C Anxious P Exuberant S Humble M

_____ S   _____ C   _____ P   _____ M

POPULAR TERMS IDENTIFYING PERSONALITY

Common Terms: Answer C	Common Terms: Answer S
Dominant Choleric Type A	**Dynamic Sanguine Expresser**
Descriptive Words:	Descriptive Words:
<ul><li>Direct</li><li>Self-propelled</li><li>Driver</li><li>Accomplishment</li><li>Accuracy</li><li>Forceful</li><li>Risk Taker</li><li>Self-reliant</li><li>Leadership</li><li>Adventurous</li><li>Decisive</li><li>Competitive</li></ul>	<ul><li>Influential</li><li>Dynamic</li><li>Expressive</li><li>Impulsive</li><li>Emotional</li><li>Generous</li><li>Poised</li><li>Persuasive</li><li>Captivating</li><li>Enthusiastic</li><li>Friendly</li><li>Inspiring</li></ul>
Common Terms: Answer P	Common Terms: Answer M
Solid Phlegmatic Idealist	**Analytical Melancholy Systematic**
Descriptive Words:	Descriptive Words:
<ul><li>Competent</li><li>Innovative</li><li>Amiable</li><li>Receptive</li><li>Steadiness</li><li>Traditional</li><li>Modest</li><li>Considerate</li><li>Loyal</li><li>Patient</li><li>Sympathetic</li><li>Neighborly</li></ul>	<ul><li>Steadiness</li><li>Analytical</li><li>Rational</li><li>Perfectionist</li><li>Diplomatic</li><li>Sensitive</li><li>Mature</li><li>Independent</li><li>Persistent</li><li>Conscientious</li><li>Precise</li><li>Thorough</li></ul>

As you can see from the descriptive words used for each personality type, each has its own strengths. Each personality type provides specific benefits within the workplace.

A keen understanding of the situations in which your personality type works the best is the next step toward implementing your career building skills. You will want to foster a work environment that generates the highest level of successful activity for your personality type.

A secondary consideration is that you should attempt to surround yourself with individuals whose personality characteristics naturally stimulate you to perform to your optimal peak expectations.

The following pages will assist you in determining the best working environment for you and the individuals whose inherent characteristics can assist you on the pathway to success.

The final consideration is to determine the most common responses of your inherent personality type to each situation relating to your adjusting activities.

Example: Adjusting requires clear, concise activity with a fine attention to detail

Your inherent personality categorization indicates that you lack organizational and time management skills

Solution: Ensure that standard organizational systems, checklists, and schedule processes are in place to enable you to maintain the flow of the claim without missing critical elements.

DOMININANT/CHOLERIC/TYPE A PERSONALITY

A dominant or choleric personality type is often referred to as a Type A personality.

This personality is typically the easiest to identify.

> These individuals will bring exceptional focus and a drive for results to the workplace.

> A choleric or Type A personality will focus on obtaining results

> The choleric person will focus so strongly on obtaining results that they will fail to pay strict attention to the feelings and ideas of others.

To obtain the best results a choleric personality must obtain:

> Direct answers to their questions

> Freedom to perform to their best without constraints or controls

> The power and authority to implement their ideas

> A variety of tasks, which contain diverse activities

> The ability to gain prestige and advancement for their activities

> Challenge

When properly focused the choleric personality will provide:

> Immediate results

> Exceptional problem solving skills and group leadership

> Quick decisions

> Focused action and project attention

When you determine that you are a choleric personality, you will need to pair yourself with individuals who can provide a balance to the strong drive inherent to the Type A personality. This will assist you in functioning at your most effective level.

Partners and groups working with a choleric should include individuals who:

Use caution.

Promote structure.

Use practical experience.

Pace themselves and others

DYNAMIC/SANGUIN/EXPRESSOR PERSONALITY

A dynamic or sanguine personality type is often referred to as an expresser or performer personality.

This personality is typically the center of a group.

> These individuals will perform vital functions to put others at ease with the goal of influencing or persuading others to view projects, tasks, and activities from their prospective.

> A dynamic or sanguine personality will focus on motivating and influencing people.

> The sanguine person occasionally focuses so strongly on the social interactions and the impression others have of them that they will loose track of time.

To obtain the best results a sanguine personality must obtain:

> Recognition and positive reinforcement

> Social situations and group projects

> Freedom to express themselves

When properly focused the sanguine personality will provide:

> Enthusiasm

> Motivation and positive attitudes in team projects or group situations

> Group participation

> Democratic policies that include mentoring and coaching

As a sanguine personality, you will function at your best when paired with individuals who can provide a balance to the focus on appearance and personality.

Partners and groups working with a sanguine should include individuals whom

Implement time management technique.

Prioritizes tasks

Use logic and planning for task management.

Speak directly.

SOLID/PHLEGMATIC/IDEALIST PERSONALITY

A phlegmatic or idealist personality type is often referred to as a solid or amiable personality.

> This personality is typically the most cooperative individual and will expend great focus on the execution of each task.

> These individuals will bring team building skills, task management follow-through and a solid dependable routine to the workplace.

> A solid or phlegmatic personality will focus on the methodical completion of a task and group cooperation.

> The idealist person will focus so strongly on the details of a particular task; they will need validation of the worth of their efforts.

> The solid personality often requires discussion concerning how their efforts contribute to the project as a whole.

To obtain the best results a solid personality must obtain:

> Sincere appreciation for your efforts

> Standard routines and clearly outlined procedures

> Guidelines for accomplishing tasks and encouragement of creative endeavors

When properly focused the idealist personality will provide:

> Consistent work output

> Stability and a calming influence in group situations

> A sincere desire to assist others

> Minimal conflict and intense identification with a group

As an idealist personality, you function at your best when paired with individuals who are of a similar level of competence. The partners of an individual with an idealist personality must have the ability to assist in prioritizing tasks and moving projects toward completion.

Partners and groups working with an idealist should include individuals who:

Implement time management technique

Prioritizes tasks

Use logic and planning for task management

Promote recognition of the group's accomplishments

ANALYTICAL/MELONCHOLY/SYSTEMATIC PERSONALITY

A melancholy or systematic personality type is often referred to as an analytical or conscientious individual.

This personality is typically the most dedicated to ensuring quality and accuracy in the completion of each task.

These individuals will bring analytical thinking, diplomacy and an attention to detail to each task and to the office.

To work best this personality type must understand the motivating factors that affect their performance.

A systematic or melancholy personality will focus on the quality and accuracy of each project or task and will work with groups to ensure diplomatic relations are maintained.

The systematic person will focus so strongly on the details of a task that they will lose focus of the overall project.

To obtain the best results a choleric personality must obtain:

Clearly defined goals and expectations

A reserved and professional atmosphere with minimal conflict

Recognition for specific skills and accomplishments

When properly focused the idealist personality will provide:

Diplomacy and a cooperative attitude with a group

Focused attention to details and standards

Critical analysis of personal and group performance

Respect for the worth of individuals as well as their accomplishments

As a systematic personality, you will function at your best when paired or working with individuals who are able to make decisions quickly. The partners of an individual with a systematic personality must have the ability to assist in prioritizing tasks and delegating specific aspects of the task.

Partners and groups working with an idealist should include individuals who:

Decisively determine direction and focus

Look beyond guidelines to promote creative activity

Initiate group discussion ensuring all parties maintain involvement in the project

Encourage team-building attitudes

Each personality defined in the previous pages contains specific strengths that apply to the position of a property claims adjuster. Each personality defined in the previous pages has inherent qualities that will require conscious modification efforts so that you have the ability to ensure the smooth adjustment and settlement of each claim assignment that you receive. Some of the most fundamental skills of successful claims adjusters include:

- **Active Listening:** Focus full attention to what other people are saying, taking time to understand the points that are being made, and asking clarifying questions as appropriate

- **Comprehension:** Read, listen, and understand information and ideas presented through written and spoken words and sentences

- **Control:** The adjuster must strive to maintain control of situations, emotions, and conversations

- **Critical Thinking:** Apply logic and reasoning skills to identify the strengths and weaknesses of alternative solutions, conclusions, or approaches to problems

- **Decision Making:** Assess the relative costs and benefits of each potential claim settlement or situational issue and respond appropriately

- **Deductive Reasoning:** Apply general rules to specific problems to produce the most sensible response or resolution

- **Detail Orientation:** An attention to the fine details of the claims adjusting and settlement process must be brought to ensure fair and timely settlement

- **Inductive Reasoning:** Correlate individual elements of information to form general rules or conclusions

- **Negotiation:** Navigating all of the elements of the claim to bring the settlement to a conclusions that is fair to both the insured and the insurer

- **Perceptiveness:** Maintaining an aware of the reactions of all parties to the loss and understanding the stimulus behind the reactions

- **Time Management:** Managing your time and the flow of the adjusting process to ensure a timely settlement of the claim

- **Verbal Communication:** Communicate knowledge, details, information, and ideas orally so that the listener gains a comprehensive understanding of the matter being defined

- **Written Communication:** Communicate knowledge, details, information, and ideas in written form so that the listener gains a comprehensive understanding of the matter being defined

Each category of the personality lends itself to one or more of the fundamental skills of the adjusting profession. Some base qualities that correlate well to the requirements of a property claims adjuster may be fostered through enhanced training, attention to ensuring skill set mastery, and administrative support that provides the companion traits that offset the inherent personality characteristics of your categorization. If you employ active learning and refine each essential skill of the adjusting profession, you will note a shift in the specifics of your testing results over time.

The application of inherent personality traits to the required skills for an insurance adjuster is essential to your career success.

INSURANCE – PROPERTY CLAIM ADJUSTING

Glossary of Terms

Actual Cash Value: The value of an item after the application of depreciation calculations The amount of money that a well-informed buyer would pay and a well-informed seller would accept for the transfer of an item within the general market

Additional Insured: An individual or entity that is not included as an insured under the insurance policy of another, but may be entitled to a certain degree of insurance protection

Additional Living Expense: The reimbursement to the insured for increased living costs when loss of his property forces him to maintain temporary residence elsewhere

Adjuster: A representative of the insurer who seeks to determine the extent of the insurer's liability for loss when a claim is submitted

Adjusting: The investigation process of settling claims by an insurance company

Agent: A licensed person or organization authorized to sell insurance by or on behalf of an insurance company

Application: A signed statement of facts made by a person applying for insurance   The application is used by the insurance company to decide whether or not to issue a policy   The application becomes part of the insurance contract when the policy is issued

Appraisal: An assessment by an independent claims appraiser estimating the amount of damage to property and the cost to repair

Arbitration Clause: A provision in a Property Insurance contract that states that if the insurer and insured cannot agree on an appropriate claim settlement, each will appoint an appraiser, and these will select a neutral umpire

A decision by any two of the three prescribes a settlement and binds both parties to it

Arson: The willful and malicious act of burning, or attempt to burn, any structure or property, usually with criminal or fraudulent intent

Broad Form: A term used to designate policies that provide insurance for multiple types of perils over and above the usual basic perils

Cancellation: The termination of insurance coverage

Claim: A request by the insured to the insurer for the settlement of a loss that is a covered peril

Claimant: The person who asserts right of coverage for a loss

Clause: Sentences and paragraphs describing coverage, exclusions, duties of an insured, and termination of coverage, and other matters relating to the insurance

Concealment: Failure of an applicant to reveal a material fact to the insurance company

Concurrent Causation: A term referring to two or more perils acting at the same time to cause a loss

Concurrent Insurance: Two or more policies with the same conditions and coverage that cover the same interest in the same property

Conditions: Provisions stated in an insurance contract that state the rights and duties of the insured or insurer

Consequential Loss: An indirect loss arising out of the policyholder's inability to use the property over a period of time, as opposed to a direct loss that happens almost instantaneously

Coverage: The protection provided under an insurance policy In property insurance, coverage lists perils insured against, properties covered, locations covered, individuals insured, and the limits of indemnification

Debris Removal Clause: A provision that may be included in a property policy to provide the insured with coverage for expenditures incurred in the removal of debris produced by an insured peril

Declarations: Page of insurance policy that details information such as name, description, and location of insured property, premiums payable, coverage amounts

Deductible: The amount of the loss which the insured is responsible to pay before benefits from the insurance company are payable

Depreciation: A decrease in value due to age, wear and tear, useful life, etc.

Direct Loss: A financial loss that results directly from an insured peril

Endorsement: Amendment to the policy used to add or delete coverage Also referred to as a rider

Exclusion: Clause or paragraph of an insurance contract that excludes coverage of certain matters

Extended Coverage: An extension of insurance coverage beyond coverage for fire and lightning

Fire Department Service Clause: A clause within an insurance policy that payment for charges resulting from action by a fire department

Fire Insurance: Coverage for damage to a dwelling or personal property as a result of a fire peril

Hazard: A matter that increases the likelihood or probable severity of a loss

Homeowner's Insurance: A property insurance contract that provides insurance against a combination of the risks of owning a home

Increased Hazard: A situation where the potential for a loss resulting from a covered peril is increased through the actions of the homeowner beyond the potential that existed at the time the policy was issued

Independent Insurance Adjuster: Individual hired by insurance companies to complete loss on an as needed basis to determine the extent of the insurer's liability for loss when a claim is submitted

Inflation-Guard: Endorsement added to a homeowner's policy to increase the face amount of insurance of the dwelling and other policy coverage's by a specified percentage to encompass the increase in costs resulting from inflation

Insurable Interest: Interest in property that dictates that a peril could cause a financial loss

Insurance: A system that enables individuals, businesses, and other organizations or entities, to pay a specified amount of money (premium) in exchange for the right to receive compensation for losses resulting from the covered perils incorporated into the policy

Insurance Adjuster: A representative of the insurer who seeks to determine the extent of the insurer's liability for loss when a claim is submitted

Insured: Policyholder other others protected in case of a covered loss or claim

Insurer: Insurance Company

Intentional Acts: Deliberate, fraudulent acts or omissions

Liability: Legally enforceable act or obligation

Limit: The maximum coverage amounts that an insurance company will provide as compensation to an insured for a covered peril

Loss: The reduction in the value of an insured's property caused by a covered peril

Loss Control: Any actions intended to reduce the frequency or severity of losses

Loss of Use Coverage: Compensation for the expenses incurred when a policyholder loses the use of their property as a result of a covered peril

Misrepresentation: The action of an applicant in making a false statement of any important fact on the application for insurance or relating to a loss claim

Mortgagee: Mortgage holder who lends money to an individual or entity in exchange for security within the subject property for the value of the mortgage

Mortgagor: Individual or entity who receives money from a lender in exchange for a security interest in a property

Mortgagee Clause: A clause in an insurance policy that protects the security interest of a mortgagee to a property jointly and separately from the named insured

Named insured: Individual, business or organization that is identified on the policy declarations page as the insured under a policy

Named Perils: Perils specifically covered on insured property

Negligence: The failure to use the reasonable care that a prudent person would have used under the same or similar circumstances

Occurrence: An event that results in an insured loss

Other Structures: Additional structures beyond the primary dwelling erected on an insured parcel of land. These structures are separated from an insured dwelling by a clear space, or are connected only by a fence or utility line

Peril: The cause of a possible loss

Personal Property: Any property of an insured other than real property

Physical Damage: Actual damage to property

Policy: Written contract of insurance

Policy Limit: The maximum coverage provided under the insurance contract

Policy Rider: An amendment, addition, or exclusion to an insurance policy that becomes a part of the contract between the insured and insurer

Policy Term: The period of time that an insurance policy provides coverage

Policyholder: The individual named on the policy as the primary insured

Premium: The amount of money an insurance company charges for insurance coverage

Proof of Loss: A sworn statement that must be furnished by the insured to an insurer before any loss under a policy may be paid

Property Insurance: Insurance that provides monetary coverage to a person with an interest in physical property for damages or a loss due to a covered peril

Provision: A clause, sentence, or paragraph of an insurance contract that describes or explains a feature, benefit, exclusion, condition, or requirement of the applicable coverage

Public Adjuster: Representative retained by the insured to protect their interested in the settlement of a claim

Reimbursement: Payment of the expenses actually incurred as a result of a peril covered by the policy

Rental Insurance: Insurance that provides coverage for the personal property of a renter or tenant in a building

Replacement Cost: The dollar amount needed to replace damaged personal property or a dwelling without deducting for depreciation

Rider: Also termed an endorsement An amendment to a policy to add or exclude specific coverage

Risk: The chance of loss

Settlement: Claim payment

Smoke Damage: Damage caused by the smoke from a fire

Stated Amount: Agreed amount of insurance

Subrogation: The process when an insurance company seeks reimbursement from another company or person for a claim it has already paid.

Term: A period of time that a policy provides coverage

Theft Limit: Special maximum limitations of coverage for certain items of personal property that incur a loss resulting from an act of theft

Trade Fixtures: Items installed within a property for use in the operation of a business

Valued Policy Law: A law that dictates that the full amount of coverage being paid for by the insured be provided as settlement if the claim is deemed a total loss without regard to the actual value of the property

Waiver: Giving up a right or privilege

APPENDIX B
ADJUSTER LICENSE REQUIREMENTS

State	License / Exam Required	Notes
Alabama	Yes	
Alaska	Yes	
Arkansas	Yes	
Arizona	Yes	
California	Yes	Non-resident adjusters may be not be licensed as a public adjuster
Colorado		
Connecticut	Yes	
Delaware	Yes	Examination requirement may be waived if adjuster holds license in a reciprocating state
District of Columbia		
Florida	Yes	
Georgia	Yes	
Hawaii	Yes	Examination requirement may be waived if adjuster holds license in a reciprocating state
Idaho	Yes	
Illinois		
Indiana		
Iowa		
Kansas		
Kentucky	Yes	
Louisiana		
Massachusetts	Yes	
Maryland		
Maine	Yes	

Michigan	Yes	Examination requirement may be waived if adjuster holds license in a reciprocating state
Minnesota	Yes	Examination requirement may be waived if adjuster holds license in a reciprocating state
Missouri		
Mississippi	Yes	
Montana	Yes	
Nebraska		
New Hampshire	Yes	
New Jersey		
New Mexico	Yes	
New York	Yes	
North Carolina	Yes	Examination requirement may be waived if adjuster holds license in a reciprocating state
North Dakota		Examination requirement may be waived if adjuster holds license in a reciprocating state
Ohio		
Oklahoma	Yes	
Oregon	Yes	
Pennsylvania		
Rhode Island	Yes	
South Carolina	Yes	
South Dakota		
Tennessee		
Texas	Yes	
Utah		
Virginia		

Vermont	Yes
Washington	Yes
Wisconsin	
Wyoming	Yes

Information entered into the chart is deemed accurate at the time of printing. All data is extracted from the issuance of the applicable state governing agency and is included for the convenience of the reader. Please contact the governing body in your state for additional details regarding licensure requirements, pre-requisites, and potential exemptions.